LORD, HELP MY UNBELIEF

LORD, HELP MY UNBELIEF

Experiencing God through Faith

Michael Rogness

RESOURCE *Publications* • Eugene, Oregon

LORD, HELP MY UNBELIEF
Experiencing God through Faith

Copyright © 2009 Michael Rogness. All rights reserved. Except for brief quotations in critical publications or reviews, no part of this book may be reproduced in any manner without prior written permission from the publisher. Write: Permissions, Wipf and Stock Publishers, 199 W. 8th Ave., Suite 3, Eugene, OR 97401.

Resource Publications
A Division of Wipf and Stock Publishers
199 W. 8th Ave., Suite 3
Eugene, OR 97401

www.wipfandstock.com

ISBN 13: 978-1-60608-051-1

Manufactured in the U.S.A.

To all the young people (and some not so young) whose questions led to this book

Contents

Introduction ix

1. The Wonder of It All 1
2. Faith in Modern Life 11
3. Faith as Trust 22
4. Obstacles to Faith 29
5. Through Doubt to Faith 43
6. Where to Start? 54
7. I Believe in God . . . the Father 66
8. I Believe in God . . . the Son 76
9. I Believe in God . . . the Holy Spirit 88
10. How Then Shall We Live? 99
11. Why the Church? 110
12. What About Heaven? 122
13. The Adventure of It All 131

Introduction

And they brought the boy to Jesus. When the spirit saw him, immediately it convulsed the boy, and he fell on the ground and rolled about, foaming at the mouth.

Jesus asked the father, "How long has this been happening to him?"

And he said, "From childhood. It has often cast him into the fire and into the water, to destroy him; but if you are able to do anything, have pity on us and help us."

Jesus said to him, "If you are able! All things can be done for the one who believes."

Immediately the father of the child cried out, "I believe, help my unbelief!"

(Mark 9:20–24, NRSV)

THIS STORY could be written today. The father of the sick boy in Mark 9 is like us. He brings his suffering son to Jesus for healing, but is unsure about his own faith. When Jesus says that faith makes things possible, he answers, "I believe, help my unbelief."

We want to believe, but sometimes we don't know how to believe or what to believe in. We wish God were more real to us. How can we experience God? How can we believe? We believe some things, we doubt some things, we wonder about a lot of things. Some days we believe more strongly than others, and there are days when we wonder if we believe anything at all. We are a curious mixture of "belief" and "unbelief."

Are you are longing for something beyond yourself that you can experience and believe in? Do you long for a genuine and personal experience of God's presence?

The purpose of this book is to help you meet God through faith. I cannot "argue" anybody into faith or "prove" faith. This book is not an argument, but rather a personal testimony. These chapters describe my own experience and the experience of others I've been with. I truly believe that the experience of God adds a brightness to life that one could not have imagined before!

First we explore the nature of faith. Then we will understand how the experience of God through faith colors and changes us forever. Much more could be written about any of these topics, but it is my hope that the suggestions given in this slim book will help you experience the wonder of living in the good news of all God has done for us!

1

The Wonder of It All

> Twinkle, twinkle, little star
> How I wonder what you are![1]

IN THE late astronomer Carl Sagan's novel *Contact,* space scientist Dr. Ellen Arroway was a "wonder junkie," because she viewed life with a sense of constant wonder. As she gazed into the night sky she thought of others who had been caught up by a sense of wonder—

> ... a tribesman seeing the magnificence of ancient Babylon for the first time, a boy from the Brooklyn slums visiting the World's Fair, Pocahontas sailing up the Thames estuary with London spread out from horizon to horizon. She even thought of Dorothy catching her first glimpse of the vaulted spires of the Emerald City of Oz. What wonders this world is full of![2]

A Christian is a "wonder junkie" too. Experiencing God in faith throws open the narrow confines of our earth-bound vision, and the world becomes full with new possibilities and vistas.

1. English poet Jane Taylor, 1806.
2. Carl Sagan, *Contact* (New York: Simon & Schuster), 1985, 322.

How can one experience God? One good place to start is a sense of wonder.

Saint Brendan was a courageous missionary to the Celtic people of ancient Britain. According to tradition Brendan was asked by the fearsome Celtic King Breda, "If I follow your Christ and become Christ's man, what will happen to me?" Saint Brendan replied, "You will stumble upon wonder upon wonder, and every wonder true!"

That's what Christianity brings into the world and into our lives!

SEEING

"I'm bored!" Who hasn't said that? We are surrounded with marvelous things which previous generations never even dreamed about, and we're often bored.

Boredom comes from limited vision. Those who appreciate and are fascinated by the world around them are not bored. The opposite of boredom is wonder—being able to see all the wonderful things in this world.

We often see very little of what goes around us. Our surroundings are teeming with life and drama. Our neighbors probably have fascinating stories from their lives, but often we are not interested enough in other people to inquire about the drama in their lives. The world of nature is brimming with life and beauty, but we can walk by a bed of roses or a fragrant lilac bush in full bloom hardly noticing, because we're in a hurry to get someplace.

The late writer Flannery O'Connor believed that her faith gave vision to her writing. "For the fiction writer, to believe nothing is to see nothing," she wrote.[3] To a friend who had left the church and her faith she wrote:

> Without faith to get beyond yourself, life remains small and fenced in. Faith opens the windows of our limited life and allows us to see further than we ever dreamed of.[4]

We modern people know an enormous amount of facts about the universe around us, but knowing is not yet wonder. Walt Whitman described the difference in his poem:

> When I heard the learn'd astronomer,
> When the proofs, the figures, were ranged in columns before me,
> When I was shown the charts and diagrams, to add, divide, and measure them,
> When I, sitting, heard the astronomer where he lectured with much applause in the lecture-room,
> How soon unaccountable I became tired and sick,
> Till rising and gliding out I wander'd off by myself,
> In the mystical moist night-air, and, from time to time,
> Looked up in perfect silence at the stars.

You might know a lot about astronomy, but the real wonder of astronomy is to go out at night and trace the path from the Big Dipper's pointer stars to the North Star, to watch the bril-

---

3. Flannery O'Connor, *The Habit of Being* (New York: Random House, a Vintage book, 1980), 147.
4. Ibid.

liant red giant Antares rise in the southern summer sky, and to spot a satellite's stately path across the sky. That's wonder!

I love astronomy, and when I'm away from city lights I spend a few minutes every night looking at the sky. Astronomy lets us know how small we are, yet how amazing it is that the God who made all that also made me and knows me! That thought never ceases to fill me with wonder! Three thousand years ago King David thought the same thing when he wrote Psalm 8:

> O LORD, our Sovereign, how majestic is your name
>   in all the earth!
> When I look at your heavens, the work of your fingers,
> the moon and the stars that you have established;
> what are human beings that you are mindful of
>   them, mortals that you care for them?
> Yet you have made them a little lower than God,
> and crowned them with glory and honor.
> You have given them dominion over the works of
>   your hands;
> you have put all things under their feet . . .
> O LORD, our Sovereign, how majestic is your name
>   in all the earth!

When we look at God's vast universe, it's awesome to think that this Creator God has come to us and made us his own people!

SEEING SIGNS OF GOD

At first Moses saw only a burning bush. As he peered more closely, astonished to realize the bush was unaffected by the flames, he heard God's voice. For English poet Elizabeth Barrett Browning that story in Exodus 3 tells us that the ordinary things of this world are full of reminders of God's presence and work, if only we look for them:

> ... Earth's crammed with heaven
> And every common bush afire with God;
> But only he who sees takes off his shoes,
> The rest sit round it and pluck blackberries.[5]

Moses recognized the presence of God and removed his shoes. Others would only have seen a burning bush.

Gregory Ojakangas, one of my former confirmation students in Duluth, Minnesota, earned his PhD in astro-physics from the California Institute of Technology. His dissertation topic was an analysis of the planet Jupiter's moons. His study led him to a sense of wonder as he thought about a God who created this world. His PhD dissertation begins with his "Acknowledgements":

> My first thanks go to God, in whom I believe and trust, for creating me, and allowing me the privilege of contemplating (in a small way) the dynamics of the Jupiter system—a part of His creation which is of unparalleled and astounding beauty, three unique and beautiful moons, each the size of a planet, whose orbits are synchronized like clockwork. It is a reality that will never grow dull for me. I feel like a very small child to whom was given a marvelous rattle to play with, a cleverly crafted thing of gyroscopes and wheels within wheels, a work which could only have been crafted by the greatest Artist of all.

---

5. Elizabeth Barrett Browning, "Aurora Leigh," in *The World's Great Religious Poetry* (New York: The Macmillan Company, 1923), 107.

That's not just science. It's wonder!

A BIGGER WORLD

Experiencing God brings wonder into our life.

The late Swedish diplomat Dag Hammarskjöld believed that the key to wonder is to realize that we are part of this world God created. "God does not die on the day when we cease to believe in a personal deity," he wrote, "but we die on the day when our lives cease to be illumined by the steady radiance, renewed daily, of a wonder, the source of which is beyond all reason."[6]

Experiencing God is like taking the blinders off a horse. Suddenly the horse sees twice as much, rather than just what is directly in front. With faith you can see further and notice things you never saw before. It's like a color-blind person suddenly being able to see in color.

I forgot the name of the movie where one of the characters said, "I have such a little life," but I thought that sentence expresses how many people feel. "Such a little life"—no wonder there.

THE WONDER OF "ORDINARY" LIFE

The astonishing thing about experiencing God is that our everyday life becomes richer, no matter who or where we are.

Is everyday life boring? Many people fill their time with all sorts of entertainment because they're bored. We love "action" movies, because they bring pizzazz into our everyday

---

6. Dag Hammarskjöld, *Markings* (New York: Alfred A. Knopf, 1964), 56.

lives. We play computer games with the illusion that our lives are caught up in the action on the screen, when all we're really doing is moving the stick or punching buttons. We "go out" to have a good time.

The truth is that there is as much drama and interest in family life as in any TV show, movie or book. Meryl Streep won acclaim portraying one of the three unhappy women in "The Hours," a film version inspired by Virginia Wolff's novel *Mrs. Dalloway*. One result of portraying such melancholy on the screen was that she appreciated her own real life much more. She hoped viewers would have the same reaction:

> I hope they have the reaction that I did, which is to feel the sharpness of *experience* and, you know, how wonderful *living* is. Even though we walk around whining or in despair or in trouble for different reasons, I thought about just how beautiful it is to love someone and to be *in your life,* the day-to-dayness of it.[7]

The most frequently performed stage play in American high schools is Thornton Wilder's *Our Town*, probably because it requires no expensive stage settings to produce it. The first two acts depict ordinary people in an ordinary New England town living ordinary lives—getting up in the morning, rushing through breakfast, greeting the milkman, going off to school and jobs, dating, falling in love, getting married, and so on.

We viewers begin to wonder, "Why did I spend money to see on stage what I live through every day?"

---

7. Quoted in Newsweek, December 9, 2002, 79.

How unsuspecting we are for the powerful impact of the play's third act! It begins with about a dozen people sitting in rows on the stage, portraying people buried in the town cemetery.

Soon Emily arrives, the schoolgirl and bride of the first two acts, who has died in childbirth. Taking an empty chair and talking to the others, she learns that one can return to life for a day. Emily chooses to return and live her twelfth birthday over again. She watches as the day begins, much like we had seen in the first act.

It's all so ordinary, just like our everyday lives. But suddenly we see it in a totally new way. We realize how precious each day is. We have only one life to live, and we're in the midst of it—each day. We are surrounded with people whom we fiercely love, yet we go about our business taking it all for granted.

As Emily plays her part, reliving her birthday and watching those around her, she is lost in wonder. She looks longingly at her mother and pleads, "Oh, Mama, just look at me one minute as though you really saw me. Mama, fourteen years have gone by. I'm dead. You're a grandmother, Mama. I married George Gibbs, Mama . . . But, just for a moment now we're all together. Mama, just for a moment we're happy. *Let's look at one another.*"

She watches as her father comes home with her birthday present in his pocket. Suddenly she can't stand it any longer and bursts out, "I can't. I can't go on. It goes so fast. We don't have time to look at one another." She breaks down sobbing,

> I didn't realize. So all that was going on and we never noticed. Take me back—up the hill—to my grave. But first: Wait! One more look. Good-by,

> Good-by, world. Good-by, Grover's Corners . . .
> Mama and Papa. Good-by to clocks ticking . . .
> and Mama's sunflowers. And food and coffee. And
> new-ironed dresses and hot baths . . . and sleeping
> and waking up. Oh, earth, you're too wonderful for
> anybody to realize you.

When Emily returns to the cemetery she asks, "Do any human beings ever realize life while they live it?—every, every minute?"

"No," is the answer. "The saints and poets, maybe . . . they do some."[8]

We in the audience who had watched the "ordinary life" of the first two acts suddenly found ourselves deeply moved. Thornton Wilder planned it that way all along. The master dramatist had portrayed everyday life, knowing that we take our daily life for granted, but how precious it is! Then in the third act, when life is over and one looks back, we realize how wonderful even those ordinary days were.

GOD AS THE SOURCE OF ALL LIFE AND WONDER

When we look at the grandeur of the creation around us, we wonder, "What's behind all this?" That question opens us to experience the Creator of it all. When we look carefully at the life of Jesus of Nazareth, we are also struck by the wonder of what he said and did. And when we trust that God's Spirit is with us always, it is a wonderful anchor to live by.

---

8. Thornton Wilder, *Our Town* (New York: HarperCollins Perennial Classic, 1938), 107–8.

That's the Christian God in a nutshell—God as Father, Son and Holy Spirit. Now we ask ourselves, "How does that God become part of our life?" How do we experience God in faith?

2

Faith in Modern Life

"You deal in faith. I live by facts."
—Spouse of one of my church members, explaining to me why he doesn't share his wife's faith.

THE MAN who said that to me grew up in church. He was a successful businessman, active in the community, a good husband and a fine father of three children. He was a splendid human being, but he quit going to church. After awhile any trace of religious faith faded from his life.

"Religion is outdated," he said to me. "It belongs to the days of superstition, before we knew what caused things. Now we know. We don't need God to explain how things work."

Polls tell us that a huge majority of Americans believe there is a God, maybe 85–90%. But is God "real" for them in their daily lives? Many people say they're "spiritual but not religious." The word "religion" has an unpleasant sound to them, and they no longer belong to or attend church.

Even among that large majority who believe in God, many have questions about what they believe.

The man who came to Jesus in Mark 9 sounds like a 21st century person. His son was tormented with an agonizing illness. Jesus said to him, "All things can be done for a person who believes." The father, desperate that his son be healed, replied, "I believe, Lord, help my unbelief!"

That's us. Most of us believe something, but we wonder about a lot of things. How do we connect with God in this modern age?

THIS NEW WORLD OF SCIENCE

If biblical people were time-warped into today's world, they would think they were on a whole different planet. They would see and hear things they never dreamed of in their wildest imagination.

Ancient science was based on what people saw. Because the sun rose in the east and set in the west, naturally they assumed the sun and the other heavenly objects moved around the earth. Lightening and thunder came from above and frightened them, so they assumed that whatever power was "up there" was angry and hurled the bolts earthward.

Ancient people thought that God, or the gods, constantly meddled in or even directed human lives. Today we explain all those areas of human life with no reference to God or divine intervention. We understand astronomy, physics, chemistry and other physical sciences to an extent undreamed of earlier. Even areas of study dealing with human beings are analyzed and explained without reference to God—biology, psychology, sociology, economics, etc.

The man described at the beginning of the chapter had become "secularized," that is, the only real world for him was this secular world, what we see, touch and hear around us. He believes that we human beings can live without God altogether. How can he and others like him come to "believe in" and "experience" God?

THE TRAUMA OF HISTORY

Secular science is not the only thing that has shaken people's faith in God. Events in recent history have deeply disturbed people's thinking about God. We think of the calculated killing of Jews in the Holocaust, the slaughter of millions in Russia, China, Cambodia, Rwanda, Bosnia, Iraq and many other places, and we wonder what God is doing and even if there is a God. "For many the huge obstacle in the path of traditional faith is the seeming impassiveness of God at the gates of Auschwitz," wrote Rabbi Harold Schulweis.[1]

Elie Wiesel grew up in a devout Jewish home in Hungary. In 1944 at the age of fourteen he was crammed into a railroad boxcar and shipped to Auschwitz along with his parents and three sisters. He experienced the horror of the Holocaust, including the death of his parents and youngest sister. Surrounded by this terrible suffering and death, he heard some Jews reciting the *Kaddish*, the prayer for the dead. As they prayed, "May the Lord's Name be blessed and magnified," young Elie rebelled:

> For the first time, I felt revolt rise up in me. Why should I bless His name? The Eternal, Lord of the Universe, the All-Powerful and Terrible, was silent. What had I to thank him for?[2]

1. Harold Schulweis, *For Those Who Can't Believe. Overcoming the Obstacles to Faith* (New York: HarperCollins, 1994), 140.

2. Elie Wiesel, *Night* (New York: Bantam Books, 1982), 31.

Elie Wiesel survived the death camps and later coined the word "Holocaust" to describe the Nazi plan to exterminate all Jews. He has become a spokesman for others whose faith in God was shattered by the horrors of that experience.

All these tragedies of suffering, cruelty and injustice around the world have caused a crisis of faith not only among Jews, but also among Christians. We ask, "Where was God in all this?" "Why didn't God do something to stop it?" "Where is God in times of suffering?" How can there be a God in a world where people kill themselves and others by smashing airplanes into buildings or blowing themselves up?

These same questions hit us on a very personal level many times in our lives. Why did God let my beautiful teenage cousin and her two brothers die of brain tumors? Why didn't God prevent that truck from killing my brother?

Finally we wonder, "Does God do *anything* in this world today?" "Is there anybody up there listening to me, or do my prayers just fly up into thin air?"

These questions have been asked since the beginning of time, but they are particularly urgent in our time. In the face of these questions many people abandoned their faith in God. Even those who kept their faith had to rethink their assumptions about God.

That's why so many people today cry out with the father in Mark 9, "Lord, help my unbelief"!

A CONFLICT OF OPPOSITES?

Many people see science and religion as opposites that contradict each other. They believe that science has made religion a relic of a by-gone era. "Take your choice," they say, "believe in religion or science, but as for me, I don't need religion to explain the world around me."

Christians believe that science and religion, or "secular" and "sacred," are both very much part of every human life, no matter how "modern" or "secular" we humans become. A friend of mine, who is a scientist and a Christian, said, "When conflicts appear between science and religion, it's a result either of bad science or of bad religion." Scientists might make statements about religion which are beyond their scientific expertise, or religious persons might make statements about science without knowing much about science.

Science and religion belong together, to enable us to understand the full richness of human life. Albert Einstein, perhaps the greatest scientist of the past century, said, "Science without religion is lame, religion without science is blind."

A DRAMATIC TURN-AROUND

In the midst of all these challenges to the Christian faith, a renewed interest in religion is occurring among today's scientists. Author and editor Gregg Easterbrook wrote that " . . . the interplay of science and religion, seemingly a dead issue a decade ago, has made a comeback, now growing into one of the liveliest arenas of intellectual discourse."[3]

"SCIENCE FINDS GOD" was the banner headline on the cover of a *Newsweek* magazine a few years ago. The article stated that "something surprising is happening between those two old warhorses science and religion":

---

3. Gregg Easterbrook, *New Republic* magazine, October 12, 1998, 24.

> The achievements of modern science seem to contradict religion and undermine faith. But for a growing number of scientists, the same discoveries offer support for spirituality and hints of the very nature of God.[4]

Recent discoveries in astronomy, physics, biology and other areas are leading many scientists around the world to conclude that there is indeed a God behind it all. Scientists themselves know that science itself cannot give meaning to life. Humans need values and meaning for life, and that brings us into the realm of faith.

University of Minnesota microbiologist Paul M. Anderson collected essays from university professors throughout the country who wrote about their faith. He described his own path to faith:

> As I struggled with my own thoughts on this matter, I came to realize that science had propelled me in the direction of faith. Why then should I find the two to be in discord? Certainly there are important issues to address in the relation between science and faith, but the Christian faith has provided me with a foundation from which to answer questions that science does not answer, such as What is the meaning of life? Why are we here? How is life to be lived? and Where do the values and morals which guide a peaceful society come from?[5]

---

4. Newsweek, July 20, 1998, 46.

5. Paul M. Anderson, *Professors Who Believe. The Spiritual Journeys of Christian Faculty* (Downers Grove IL, InterVarsity Press, 1998), 22.

FACTS

We can understand the relationship between science and religion if we begin with the distinction between *facts* and *faith*.

"Facts" are truths that can be proved by physical or logical demonstration. Mathematical equations and geometrical axioms can be shown to be true. You can use your fingers to show that $6 + 3 = 9$ is true. With an accurate thermometer you can prove that water freezes at 32°F. Facts can be proved by repeated experiments and observation.

Sometimes the line between theory and fact is fuzzy. We make a judgment based on the best evidence we have, even though we cannot actually see physical evidence. We speak of "quantum mechanics," even though these tiny subatomic particles cannot be seen. Albert Einstein's theories of relativity and the relationship between energy and matter are called "theories." His theories have led most astronomers and physicists to believe in the existence of "black holes," even though nobody has actually seen one. Indeed, by their very nature they cannot be seen. Yet the evidence is so strong that astronomers speak of black holes as a fact of the universe.

But for the most part "facts are facts," as we say.

FAITH

Alongside "facts" is "faith." Faith is *living in trust that something is true or reliable, although it is beyond the realm of those facts which are "scientifically" predicted or proven.* The Bible defines faith as "the assurance of things hoped for, the conviction of things not seen." (Hebrews 11:1)

Faith is a belief, action or decision done on trust in something beyond the boundaries of scientific fact. We act on that faith, trusting that it is true. Faith is a living thing. We accept facts as true, but faith shapes how we really live.

Yes, modern science has moved many areas of knowledge of the world around us from the realm of faith into fact. As science expanded, many things about which people had given religious causes and had believed in by *faith* were now understood by the *facts* discovered by scholars.

But faith is still very much part of human life. Facts are neutral, but faith moves us into the realm of values, meaning and relationships in life.

VALUES

Facts won't determine what's important for your life. The square root of 25 is 5, and it's irrelevant whether you think that's important or not. However, when you switch to the realm of faith, then values enter the picture. Your life is shaped not by facts, but by your values.

What's important to you? Those are your values. We speak of "family values," to describe people who consider family life important. Such persons will support legislation which they think helps families stay together. If advancement in your career is more important to you than the community you live in, you will move when a better job offer comes along. If your community is more important than a job, you will take a job at less pay to stay in your hometown.

If you find a wallet on the sidewalk with $500 in it, will you return it to its owner? If you value honesty, that is, if you believe that being honest is the best way to live, you will return the wallet. If you believe it's "everyone for himself" in this world, then you will probably keep the money.

We don't make decisions about facts. They are true no matter what we believe. In the realm of faith we make decisions all the time, and those decisions are based on our values, what we think is important.

MEANING

Faith is tied not only to values, but also to one's meaning and purpose to life. Our lives are far richer than a collection of factual observations about the universe around us. They won't furnish your life with meaning.

Scientific facts of nature don't give meaning to our lives. Two people might ascribe quite different meanings to the same facts. For some people the vastness of the universe diminishes the meaning and importance of human life. Others believe that a vast universe enhances our existence as human beings. Astronomer Alan Dressler said,

> When I talk to audiences about the size and age of the cosmos, people often say, "It makes me feel so insignificant." I answer, "The bigger and more impersonal the universe is, the more meaningful you are, because this vast, impersonal place needs something significant to fill it up." We've abandoned the old belief that humanity is at the physical center of the universe, but must come back to believing we are at the center of meaning.[6]

No matter what we know or speculate about the world around us, each of us longs to find meaning for our own lives.

6. Quoted by Gregg Easterbrook, ibid., 29.

Viktor Frankl was a young psychiatrist in Austria when he and his family were arrested and sent to a concentration camp. The book he had just written was destroyed. Having lost everything, and suffering from constant hunger, cold and brutality, could there be any meaning or purpose for his life anymore?

He was determined to survive so that he could rewrite his book. As he observed the prisoners around him in the midst of appalling misery, he realized that those persons who had a reason to live, some goal to live for, some meaning in life—those people had a better chance of survival. Those who had no reason to live, no goals before them, and saw no meaning to life—they did not survive. He concluded:

> There is nothing in the world, I venture to say, that would so effectively help one to survive even the worst conditions, as the knowledge that there is a meaning in one's life . . . He who has a *why* to live for can bear almost any *how*.[7]

His desire to rewrite his book gave his life meaning and a goal. Without that he is convinced he would have given up and died.

Your life is a complicated collection of relationships among family and friends, connections to places you have lived in, past memories, hopes and dreams of what you hope to accomplish, and the list goes on. We humans are bundles of feelings which give texture to life—love, fear, compassion, courage, happiness, grief, etc. They all combine to give meaning to our lives. They put us squarely in the realm of faith and

---

7. Viktor Frankl, *Man's Search for Meaning* (New York: Washington Square Press, 1966), 164.

experience, because we live according to what we believe and trust in for meaning in our lives.

We want a faith which is alive and vital in our life. We want an experience of God which is alive and vital in our life. For that, we need to consider what faith is.

3

Faith as Trust

> A biologist spotted a rare plant below a steep precipice, but it was too dangerous for a grown person to scale down the cliff wall. He motioned to a small boy standing nearby and called to him, "You see that plant down there, sonny? If you let me tie this rope around you and lower you down to get it, I'll give you $25."
>
> The boy quickly replied, "It's a deal. But first I'll run home and get my Dad to hold the rope."

THE BOY was willing go over the cliff only if somebody he trusted held the rope. Any time we venture forth into the unknown we want to have something we trust to hold on to. That's what faith is—acting on trust.

FROM KNOWLEDGE AND AGREEMENT TO TRUST

We often make two big mistakes in thinking about faith, which make it difficult to experience God through faith.

- The first mistake is to think of faith as *a list of statements which one must believe are true*. Of course faith involves things we believe are true, but that's not what the heart of faith is.

- The second mistake is to think of faith as *a thing, something large or small.* Typical statements are, "He has a lot of faith," or, "I wish I had more faith."

Faith is trust. It is *a belief, action or decision done in trust.* We live and act on that faith, trusting that it is true.

Christian scholars have traditionally defined faith by contrasting "knowledge," "agreement" and "trust."

Faith is more than knowledge. I might *know* what the Bible says about God, but that's not faith yet. Agreement is one step toward faith, but it also isn't faith. I might not only *know* what the Bible says about God, and I might even *agree* that there is a God, but I might still live my life totally unaffected by whoever or whatever God is.

Faith is ultimately *trust.* I not only *know about* God, I not only *agree* that there is a God, but I *trust* my life to God! I live my life in the confidence that God exists, and that changes the way I think about everything.

In 1860 the French tight-wire walker Jean Francois Gravelet, known as "Blondin," announced he would walk across a wire strung above Niagara Falls. Twelve thousand curious spectators came to see him. Back and forth he walked above the thundering water. He pivoted on one leg, turned somersaults, and even pushed a wheelbarrow across. The people gasped in suspense with each new trick. One slip and he would be swept over the falls and crushed on the rocks below.

The crowd cheered and cheered. Blondin announced that he would carry another person across on his back and called for a volunteer. "Yes, yes, you can do it!" the crowd shouted, but no one volunteered. Finally he summoned his manager to climb on his back, and he carried the terrified man on his shoulders safely to the other side.

The crowd had confidence that Blondin could do it. They had *knowledge* and *agreement*, but no one had *trust* enough to entrust their lives to him!

FAITH AS PART OF EVERYDAY LIFE

Once faith is defined as trust, we realize that even in this scientific age we all live by faith every day, even people who aren't at all religious. Every day we do things, even though we cannot prove "scientifically" that they are true or reliable. In most of our decisions we gather what facts we can, but then we act in the hope or trust that it will work.

Getting into a car is an act of faith. We are trusting that our car will not break down or that an oncoming driver will not crash into us. Almost all the time our trust is justified, but every now then we read some tragic story about somebody whose trust was misplaced and was killed in an accident.

Your whole day is one act of faith after another.

- Every time you go into a restaurant, you don't have a taster sample the food before you, like paranoid rulers used to do. You "trust" that the cook is not a maniac poisoner.
- Stepping into an elevator is an act of faith.
- Being among people is an act of faith that a terrorist or murderer isn't nearby with plans to kill you.
- Just getting out of bed and starting your everyday routine is an act of faith that your body will not collapse.

However there are times when what we've trusted in proves unreliable, and our faith is misplaced.

- Cars break down 200 miles after we have set off on a long journey.
- People roar through stop signs and smash into us.
- Strange bacteria infect people in restaurants.
- Elevator cables might snap.
- People in apparent good health drop dead of heart attacks.
- Terrorists and murderers kill totally unsuspecting people waiting at a bus stop or shopping.

If somebody says, "I live my life only by facts, by what I *know* to be true scientifically," would she ever take any kind of risk? She might be head over heels in love with a young man, and he in love with her, and they might have a deliriously happy courtship. Their faith in each other seems to be well placed. By all the factors they "know"—deep friendship, common interests, shared values, etc.—they believe they are destined for a happy marriage. Can they ever "know" for sure? No. Marriage is always an act of faith.

How do you make your career choices? You might love geology—a fact you know for sure—but do you "know" there will be a job waiting for you after you receive your diploma? You hope and trust there will be, but you cannot predict or prove it at the time. Today's students may choose careers because they think there will be jobs available. Usually careful planning can be trusted, but situations might change. Ultimately the choice is made on faith.

All your big decisions in life are acts of faith! You collect all the "facts" you can, but finally you act in trust that the object of your trust will be true and reliable. If you have chosen carefully, your chances of success will be improved. But you can never know for sure.

No matter how far technology and science advance, the truth remains: Faith is always, always for everybody, a part of human life.

A wonderful old Jewish legend gives us an example of faith as trust.

> After the Exodus from Egypt, the Israelites arrived at the Red Sea, with Pharaoh's army in hot pursuit. The people stood at the shore, Moses struck his staff on the ground. But nothing happened. The waves did not part to let them through. The people could see the dust raised by Pharaoh's pursuing army coming ever nearer. Moses stretched out his hand over the sea once again, and still nothing happened. Finally one desperate Israelite plunged into the sea. Then—and only then—did the waters roll back!

That part of the Exodus story is not in the Bible, but it describes faith. God's promise to deliver the people was all that frightened man had to go on. He trusted that promise, acted on it by plunging into the waves, and his trust proved reliable.

SOURCE OF FAITH

We speak of "my faith" in God, as if it's something I decide or do. That puts the whole burden of believing on me, and I end up agonizing whether I have "any faith" or "enough faith."

Of course it is "my faith," but if we start there, we'll never get beyond the "my."

Faith is not created by itself or by the person who has faith. It is created by God, the *object* of faith! Think of the analogy of love. Do you decide to fall in love? No, you *realize* you are in love.

How did that happen?

It happened because there was something in the other person which drew you to him or her. The other person had qualities which attracted you, and you fell in love. Where did that love come from? From your decision? From your thinking? No, *that love was created by the other person*!

Love is not based on facts. Of course you will look for facts that support or explain your love: He has a wonderful personality, he loves music as I do, he likes many of the same activities, he is handsome, etc. But other people might have these same characteristics, and you did not fall in love with them. By some mystery you cannot analyze logically, you fell in love with him. It was he who aroused or created that love for him within you.

In time your own thinking, will and decisions become part of the process. At some point you recognize the attraction you are feeling for the other person and you decide to pursue it. You realize you want to spend the rest of your life with her, and you propose marriage. Your actions and decisions really all came because of her.

Faith in God is like that. Through faith we experience God becoming part of our life. God creates faith within us, a process that cannot be analyzed any easier than analyzing why we fall in love with another person.

However we are not helpless puppets after this takes place. Once faith is begun, our minds and decisions play a key part in how our lives unfold from then on.

A BIG DIFFERENCE

Faith asks two basic questions: "Is it true?" and "Does it make a difference in my life?" Or to put it more simply, faith asks: "What's what?" and "So what?"

Faith makes a huge difference. The values you hold and the meaning you find in life come from what you believe in. Faith and your experience with God will shape your life in ways that you cannot even imagine.

Nobody lives without faith. You live by what you like and consider important. Maybe you trust in comfort, pleasure, earning as much money as possible, having fun, seeking thrills, or whatever. The direction of your life is determined by what you believe in, even if you haven't consciously thought about it.

Trusting in God makes a decisive difference in one's life. Faith sometimes takes us into uncertain territory. Unexpected experiences will happen to us.

"Hitch your wagon to a star" is an old proverb. You can say it another way: "Put your faith in something really big!" Faith reaches out and hitches your life to something solid to stand on and a grand vision to steer by. You begin to experience life in a whole new way.

One thing is certain: Life with God is never routine or uninteresting! So how do I find faith and experience God?

4

Obstacles to Faith

> But it seems that something has happened that has never happened before: though we know not just when, or why, or how, or where. People have left God, not for other gods, they say, but for no god; and this has never happened before ...[1]

WHY HAVE so many modern people "left God," as English poet T. S. Eliot said more than a half-century ago? There are many reasons. I have talked with many people who have difficulty with faith, with religion, or with the church. This chapter lists some of their reasons. I suspect every reader will recognize some of his or her feelings in this list.

BORING

"Church services are boring!" How often I hear that! Truth is, I'm often bored in church myself.

Part of the problem is the difference in preferences. People who grew up with stately chorale-type hymns love them, and these hymns nourish their faith. Younger persons listen to a totally different kind of music and often find old

---

1. T. S. Eliot, Choruses from "The Rock," in *The Complete Poems and Plays* (New York: Harcourt, Brace and Company, 1952), 108.

hymns stuffy. Some people want a sermon to be a half hour long, others want them shorter.

Worship is not meant to be "entertaining," but it should not be boring. Throughout the centuries the church has adapted its worship to changing times and new cultures. Good worship keeps what is best about the past and incorporates new elements as well. Most congregations try to appeal to as many people as possible. Pick any church at random, and you will often find a book of modern songs next to the traditional worship book.

It helps to learn about worship traditions, because there are reasons for what the church has done for centuries. You can also speak to leaders in the congregation and tell them what you find boring. There is a huge variety in worship styles, and you will find one that fits you.

UNACCEPTABLE GOD

Recently a church ran a full-page ad in a national magazine with this headline: "Is God Keeping You from Going to Church?" The following sentence said, "Maybe you're uncomfortable with the idea of God—or at least someone else's idea of God." Many people think that the Christian idea of God is a stern, judging and angry being, so they want nothing to do with that kind of faith or church.

Somebody once told me, "I can't believe in a God who lets babies starve, children die of leukemia, or people be slaughtered and tortured!"

My answer was, "If that's what God is doing, I would be an atheist too." The great eighteenth-century Methodist leader John Wesley listened to a woman who believed that God frowned upon any kind of joy in life. He replied, "Madam, if that is the kind of God you believe in, then your God is my devil!"

There are plenty of things about God I find puzzling. Even in the Bible God sometimes appears mean and angry. There are lots of things I do not understand about God.

I have no easy answer to the cry, "Why didn't God DO something here?" I also have no simple explanations for many of God's apparent actions in the Bible. I'll go to heaven with a list of things to ask God.

However, there are crucially important things about God I do know, because they are in the Bible. Both Old and New Testaments speak about God as creator, as law-giver, as merciful, as caring and involved in human's lives, and finally the God who promised and sent Jesus. There are a lot of things about God which strike me as terrific good news, which deeply affect my life.

I focus on those things.

UNACCEPTABLE BIBLE

"The Bible is a terrible book. Look at those people in the Old Testament killing others to obey God!"

That's a common observation. The Bible includes both wonderful and terrible things. It doesn't whitewash the gritty areas of life at all. Life was as mean and cruel in those days as it is today, and the Bible includes that side of life too. Sometimes the authors even justify terrible deeds by saying God wanted them done. There is no Bible scholar in the world who can "explain" all these difficult verses.

Furthermore, people have used the Bible to justify cruel actions—slavery, bigamy, apartheid, race discrimination, economic oppression, war, cruel criminal punishment, and so on. I suppose that people can find something in the Bible to prove anything they want!

On the other hand, the Bible also contains words of comfort, encouragement, inspiration, strength, reconciliation, restoration and new life. For all those things I treasure the Bible, even while living with my lingering questions about troublesome verses.

One of the principles of the Reformation in the 1500s was: *Use the clear verses to explain the difficult verses.* Put another way: Build your faith on the verses of the Bible that you can understand, not on the puzzling verses. It's good advice.

IMPERFECT CHURCH

"All the church wants is money" . . . "This church is not concerned about the poor" . . . "All I do is support a bloated church bureaucracy" . . . "I don't like the polices of my church body."

We've all heard these comments, and most of us have said one or more of them.

One cynic said, "Jesus promised the Kingdom of God, and we got the church instead." The "church" as institution has all the weaknesses of other institutions.

The church has a grand vision and high ideals. But it takes people working together to accomplish them, and that probably means some boring meetings. On the national level, meetings involve airplanes, motels, rented cars and expense accounts, which take a great deal of money, and often we don't see any immediate results. That's the price for operating democratically.

Furthermore, there are groups in the church with whom I might disagree. I might be tempted just to leave and go somewhere else.

In that way the church is similar to other institutions in our society. Schools, government, legal system, social agencies, family—they all have high goals and an essential role in society. Most of the time they're made up of good people doing their best. But institutions make mistakes and do foolish things, because they're made up of fallible human beings. There are crooks and scoundrels in the church as well as in any institution, except that the misdeeds of church leaders usually hit the headlines and give a bad name to the vast majority of church workers who are dedicated.

So why be part of the church? Because the church can do things which isolated individuals cannot. As an individual I can't build and maintain schools, hospitals, homes for the elderly and children, feed hungry people in Africa, send missionaries, and publish educational materials, devotional literature and music, and so on. I can only do that as part of the church, and that means meetings and decisions that won't be unanimous.

Society can't function without institutions. None of them is ever perfect and they can always be improved, but human life needs them.

However, the church is different from other institutions. No matter what issue is being discussed, nobody can tell another church member, "You and your opinions don't count for anything." That might happen in other institutions, but it cannot happen in the church, because a basic part of the church's faith is that every person is important. You might disagree with something the church does, and you might criticize the church, but no one can discount you or diminish your value as a part of the church.

THE CHURCH'S PAST SHORTCOMINGS

Since the church is a fellowship of imperfect people, it's not hard to find instances of terrible wrongs in its history. Why didn't churches speak out more openly against Hitler and the Holocaust? Why did so many church people oppose civil rights for minorities? Why hasn't the church exerted more influence in environmental issues, to protect God's precious earth from exploitation and pollution? Why have countries with Christian majorities fought so many wars, many against each other?

These questions could go on and on. On the other side, to each question one can also find Christians who did speak out, who did work for justice, who did risk their safety to help others. My wife's family were refugees after World War Two, living temporarily in a foreign country until a congregation in South Dakota brought them to the USA and helped them resettle. The Christian churches were in the forefront of the struggle which resulted in the collapse of communist regimes in Eastern Europe. In the devastating Red River flood of 1997 in the Upper Midwest, disaster relief efforts were organized through the churches.

In any crisis of history, we find Christians who have done evil, Christians who have remained silent, and Christians who have risen up heroically, suffered and died for their convictions. A person can reject Christianity for the shortcomings of some Christians, or a person can be inspired by the courage of other Christians.

INHOSPITABLE CONGREGATION

I visit many congregations on Sunday mornings. Most of them have a "fellowship hour" following the worship service. For many people that means "fellowship with my friends," and I stand there all by myself. It's hard to break into the tight little circles of good friends talking among themselves.

A Christian congregation can be as cold and inhospitable as a medical clinic waiting room. Many of us have had the experience of going to a new church where nobody greets or talks to us. Everybody seems to know each other, but we stand by ourselves with our styrofoam coffee cup in hand and nobody comes by to say hello. It's sometimes easier to meet people in a bar than a church narthex.

There are reasons for this, of course. Many people who are by nature warm and friendly feel awkward meeting strangers.

Most congregations are working to become more hospitable. With some persistence a stranger new in town will find more friends in a short time at church than any other place in town. It helps if a newcomer volunteers for church activities.

In time people often find their closest friends within their congregation. Life in a congregation draws people together into a whole fabric of rich relationships. The church does not divide people into social and economic classes, and you can have close relationships with people in church which you would never have outside in the community. You might never meet the accountant who works down the block from you, but you become acquainted with her because she is your son's Sunday School teacher. A doctor might never become friends with the check-out lady at the grocery store, but they learn to know each other by singing in the choir together. In my first parish I picked up my mail at the post office and often met people from the congregation in the lobby or in the drugstore afterward over coffee. Being part of the congregation drew me into people's lives every day of the week all over town!

UNKIND CHRISTIANS

Rudy Baylor, the young lawyer in John Grisham's novel *The Rainmaker*, recalls his childhood when his mother was hospitalized and the ladies of their Methodist church rallied to help the family:

> . . . for three days our house was flooded with casseroles, cakes, pies, breads, pots and dishes filled with more food than my father and I could eat in a year. The ladies organized a sitting for us. They took turns supervising the food, cleaning the kitchen, greeting even more guests who brought even more casseroles . . . Our house had never felt such warmth, never seen so much delicious food. The ladies fussed over me . . . and I relished the attention. They were the aunts and grandmothers I'd never known.

Shortly after his mother returned home there was a controversy in the church. Rudy remembers, "Someone insulted my mother, and that was the end of church for us."[2] That same

---

2. John Grisham, *The Rainmaker* (New York: Doubleday, 1995), 109–10.

story can be told in thousands of households across the country: One bad experience in church and a person doesn't go anymore.

That episode in John Grisham's novel describes the best and the worst of what a Christian congregation can be. While his mother was in the hospital the ladies of the church rallied to care for the family, but one bad experience stopped their going.

A young adult told me once, "I grew up in a church where all they did was fight. I got sick and tired of it. I quit going." That happens. Sometimes Christians don't get along very well. Sometimes they fight, even in church. After all, they are human beings with the foibles and shortcomings we all have.

A person on one of our church committees was very difficult to get along with. He griped about everything and was very uncooperative. Unfortunately he almost never missed a meeting. Another long-suffering member of the group observed, "Imagine what he'd be like if he *weren't* a Christian!"

She had put her finger on a profound truth: Christians are people too, and sometimes they aren't very nice. Nobody claims Christians are finished products. God is working on us all through our lives. A friend of mine observed that, "God has a lot further to go with some of us than with others!"

There is another deep truth here: Even if and when Christians don't get along, we are still bound together by our common faith. Like it or not, we're brothers and sisters under the same God, and Jesus tells us to love one another. An elderly pastor told me once, "Jesus told us to love each other, but he didn't tell us we had to *like* everyone!"

Strange things happen in a church. One of our new members was elected to the Church Council, and after a couple meetings with lively debates, she said to me, "If I knew what went on in these meetings, I might not have joined this church. The way people argue isn't very Christian!" Six months later I asked her how she felt about Church Council. She said, "It's not so bad. I know these people now, and I can understand why they feel that way. We still argue, but we also drink coffee together afterwards."

HYPOCRITICAL CHRISTIANS

Many people reject the Christian faith because they think Christians are hypocrites.

A person told my pastor, "I don't think I'll join this congregation, because there are too many hypocrites in it!" This wise pastor replied, "Yes, there are, and there's always room for one more."

Of course there are hypocrites in the church. There are times when every one of us is hypocritical. At least we know that we are, and part of Christian living is to struggle against hypocrisy. Everyone is welcome to join in that struggle!

Every Christian is a hypocrite, because we aim higher than we can ever reach. We strive to "love our neighbors as ourselves," as Jesus told us, but we fall short.

But we know that's our goal. And Christians try.

DISAPPOINTED EXPECTATIONS

An elderly lady in our congregation once sent me a terse letter:

> Dear Pastor Rogness,
>
> Please take my name off the church membership list.
>
> Thank you very much.
> Lucille

I went to her home and rang the doorbell. She opened the door, saw me through the screen and slammed the door in my face. Later I called her friends and asked what the problem was. "We don't know," they told me, "but she's going to another church." I wrote her a note, but she never answered. Even years later, I never did find out why she left our congregation. Something must have disappointed or angered her very much. Somehow our church did not measure up to what she wanted. I can only hope that she found what she was looking for in the other church.

Many people drop out of church because they have been disappointed or disillusioned. The possibilities are endless. Maybe a member snubbed them. Maybe the pastor said something they disagreed with. Maybe the church body took a position they couldn't accept. Maybe the organist played too slowly, or the hymns were too old.

We tend to look upon the Christian church with a consumer mentality: "What's in it for me? What will I get out of it?" There is a lot in it for you, and you will get a lot out of it, but if that's our primary question, we're bound to be disappointed. What we "get out of" church is a by-product of being part of the church, not the main reason for being there.

NOT THE "RELIGIOUS TYPE," NOT INTERESTED

"I'm just not the religious type," a sharp college student said to me once. His idea of a "religious kind of person" was a pallid, washed-out, pious person who prayed a lot and went to church on Sunday and Bible study on Wednesday. If that were my idea of a "religious person," I wouldn't qualify either, and wouldn't even want to.

A Christian can't be stereotyped into one "type." They include all types. Take any adjective that might describe a person, then take an adjective describing the opposite, and you can find that kind of Christian too—quiet/noisy, introvert/extrovert, scholarly/practical, musical/tone-deaf, awkward/athletic, etc.

Don't get sidetracked by one "type" or another. Stay with the real issues of life—what's true? what's good? what's the meaning of life? how do we live? and so on. Those are the big issues of life for every human being, and those are the issues Christianity deals with. Wrestle with these, and you will discover that the issues of Christian faith are exactly the issues you face in your own life.

Another way of putting this obstacle is, "I'm not interested in religion." My immediate answer is, "I'm not either, but we're talking about Christianity, not religion." There's a difference, as we'll see later.

A person who "isn't interested in religion" has narrowed his life and cut off a whole lot of excitement and possibilities from life. Becoming a Christian is like taking the blinders off a horse. Suddenly the horse sees twice as much, rather than just what is directly in front. With faith you can see further and notice things you never saw before. Becoming Christian is like a color-blind person suddenly being able to see in color.

Rabbi Schulweis recalls a young man named David who said, "I'm not the religious type, but I am a spiritual person." David considered himself "ethnically Jewish," but left his Jewish faith and never attended synagogue services. Rabbi Schulweis wonders how long David's Jewish identity will last, now that it is separated from its foundation. "For David has no language, no song, no poetry, no drama, no Zion, no God."[3] How can a person be "spiritual" without some content or substance of faith?

We don't strive to become "religious." It's faith we're looking for, not religion. We might become "religious" in the process, but that's a by-product, not the goal.

DON'T SWEEP THEM UNDER THE RUG

These obstacles are problems, and they can be very painful experiences. But they should be faced squarely, not sidestepped or ignored.

The tragedy is that a lot of people throw the baby out with the bath water. The obstacles are real and true, so they close their minds to Christianity altogether. Or they put off decisions about faith and church membership. That's nothing new. When the Apostle Paul talked to Governor Felix and his wife Drusilla about Jesus, Felix postponed further discussion by saying, "When I have an opportunity, I will send for you." Acts 24:25) As far as we know he never did.

It's easy to find things we don't like, both in the Bible and among church people. How sad it is when a person confronts

3. Harold Schulweis, ibid., 4–5.

one of these obstacles—and we all do, perhaps many times in our life—and throws out the whole Christian faith.

5

Through Doubt to Faith

> I think there is no suffering greater than what is caused by the doubts of those who want to believe. I know what this torment is, but I can only see it, in myself anyway, as the process by which faith is deepened. A faith that just accepts is a child's faith and all right for children, but eventually you have to grow religiously as in every other way.[1]

"How can I experience God?" "How can I get faith? I would like to believe, but I can't!" These are the cries of many sincere searchers. For many it comes from the difficult transition from a childhood faith that believes without reflection to an adult faith where the deep questions of life and death are faced.

Augustine was an African who lived four hundred years after Jesus. He became a Christian as a young adult when he learned to know Ambrose, the intrepid bishop of Milan, Italy. In time Augustine himself became a leading bishop and scholar of the church. In one of his prayers he looked back on his own life and said, "The human soul is restless until it rests in you, O God."

---

1. Flannery O'Connor, ibid., 353–54.

If you feel a spiritual restlessness, you may wonder, "How does one experience God and get faith?"

The first step is: Be honest with God! Plunge in with your very toughest questions.

FROM DOUBT TO FAITH

We can use the term "lover's quarrel" to describe our relationship to God. When Canadian pastor R. Maurice Boyd was the senior minister at Fifth Avenue Presbyterian Church in New York City, he told his congregation how his faith was formed and shaped by his doubts. He too used the term "a lover's quarrel" to describe his experience:

> The story of my life is a lover's quarrel with Christian belief. I love the faith ... [But] there is hardly a doubt about Christian belief that I haven't asked. I have been vexed by every spiritual conundrum. And I have grown, not by credulity, but by skepticism ... The greatest Christians have been the greatest skeptics. I think of St. Augustine and Pascal and Kierkegaard and Swift. In our time I think of C.S. Lewis and Malcolm Muggeridge. Skeptics all, but Christians too ... Doubt is not the enemy of faith but an element in faith. I have found that doubt has illumined and enriched my faith ... I can say with Dostoevsky, "My hosanna has come forth from the crucible of my doubts." So have your doubts and continue your search, and do not feel guilty about it. Don't think you must take your doubts and uncertainties outside the church, but bring them along with you when you come![2]

2. R. Maurice Boyd, *A Lover's Quarrel with the World* (Philadelphia: Westminster Press, 1985), 17–18.

"Bring your doubts along with you" is good advice. Never be afraid of asking your questions. After all, a God who is the God of truth is not at all afraid of any questions from an honest searcher for truth. Flannery O'Connor's advice is very helpful:

> If you feel you can't believe, you must at least do this: keep an open mind. Keep it open toward faith, keep wanting it, keep asking for it, and leave the rest to God.[3]

It is a common but totally false idea that the opposite of faith is doubt. The opposite of faith is indifference or disinterest. We might call doubt the "front porch of faith," because the way to the living room of a mature faith is through the struggle of doubts and questions.

Earlier I described Elie Wiesel's crisis of faith when he witnessed the horrors of the Auschwitz death camp. A few years ago he spoke at Eckerd College in St. Petersburg, Florida. Following his speech an 8th-grade teacher told him that her students had read his novel *Night*, about the suffering at Auschwitz. They wondered, "Did he lose his faith?" Elie Wiesel answered her,

> The book was about my anger with God, not my disbelief. I quarrel with God. But after I quarrel, I pray.[4]

---

3. Flannery O'Connor, ibid., 354.
4. *Minneapolis Star-Tribune*, April 27, 1997, E4.

LIVE "AS IF"

Episcopalian priest Samuel Shoemaker was one of the founders of Alcoholics Anonymous. One of his great concerns was to help people who were searching for God and struggling with questions of faith. Almost a half century ago he wrote an article which helped so many people that it was reprinted in the *Reader's Digest*, then distributed by the thousands as a reprint. The title was "Act As If . . . " He told about a skeptic who did not know what he believed about God or prayer. Shoemaker advised him to speak honestly to whatever higher power he believed in and say exactly what was on his mind. The skeptic prayed,

O God, if there be a God, send me help now, because I need it. Amen[5]

It was a totally honest prayer. Shoemaker advised his friend to continue praying whatever was on his mind and to read a chapter from the Bible each day before bedtime. He also suggested attending church to observe the faith of other people. In time the skeptic was baptized and became a leader in his congregation.

Shoemaker's advice was very simple, yet very profound. If you feel distant from God and have trouble believing, do what Christians do: Live as Christians do, worship and pray as Christians do. Blaise Pascal, a French scientist and philosopher in the 1600s, was a devout Christian. A friend seeking God said to him, "I wish I had your faith, then I would live your life." Pascal replied, "Live my life and you will soon have my faith." A person receives faith as he or she lives the faith.

---

5. Samuel Schoemaker, *Christian Herald*, October 1954, 22.

Live "as if" God is present in your life and eventually you will experience God there.

A person never becomes a Christian by looking at faith as a spectator, as if one is watching the game from the bleachers. You can stand on the sidewalk and look at the goods in the store window, but they will never become yours until you go into the store.

You cannot "think" your way to faith. Strange as it seems, *you become a Christian by being a Christian!*

There is nothing new to this. Many things in life can be experienced only when one goes ahead and lives them. Looking at food on a plate will neither nourish you nor convince you of its taste. You have to eat it to find out if it's tasty and nutritious. Watching somebody at physical activity won't help you get into shape. You have to jog around the block or play the game yourself. You can practice swimming strokes on dry land all you want, but you won't know what it's like to swim until you plunge into the water and try it.

After surviving Auschwitz and Buchenwald as a teenager, Elie Wiesel struggled with God and faith. He was confused and enraged about God and wondered why God hadn't stopped the slaughter. Yet in all his agony he discovered that he could not ignore God:

> One can be a good Jew, or a good Christian, with God or against God, but not without God. One may be against God for the sake of His creation. I quarrel with God, fight with God and make up with God, but I am never without God.[6]

---

6. *The Journal of Higher Education*, quoted by Martin Marty in *Context*, June 1, 1983, 2.

What exactly does one *do* to experience God and "get" faith?

A VISIT IN THE NIGHT

The Jewish leader Nicodemus was a prominent leader and was probably enjoying a very good life. But something made him curious about this wandering prophet Jesus of Nazareth. Other religious leaders in Jerusalem believed Jesus was a trouble-maker, a fake, or worse, a blasphemer. Even so, Nicodemus wanted to meet Jesus. He came to Jesus one night in secret, so none of the other leaders would know about the meeting. Jesus spoke to him about being born again in God. He said,

> Do not be astonished that I said to you, 'You must be born from above.' The wind blows where it chooses, and you hear the sound of it, but you do not know where it comes from or where it goes. So it is with everyone who is born of the Spirit. (John 3:7–8)

Nicodemus knew that "wind" and "Spirit" are the same word in the Hebrew language. Jesus was saying that God's Spirit works like the wind: It blows where it will, unpredictably. God's Spirit works like the wind, blowing sometimes gently, sometimes forcefully, and nobody can predict beforehand when and where it will blow.

What had Nicodemus done to "get" faith? Simple: he came to Jesus and listened.

That furtive midnight encounter changed his whole life. He became a disciple, defended Jesus before the Pharisees and came forward to help bury Jesus's body after the crucifixion. (John 17:50; 19:39) Nicodemus had become a Christian.

DIFFERENT EXPERIENCES FOR DIFFERENT PEOPLE

What drives our quest for faith? Why do we long to experience God in our life? There are several possibilities.

1. A personal need. It might be a burden of guilt, a resentment or anger which won't go away, a fear of the future, a crushing financial crisis, a moral failure, a yearning to belong to something or somebody—anything that makes a person realize a desperate need in one's life. Such needs can lead to God. The first rule of Alcoholics Anonymous is that our life has become unmanageable and we need God.

2. The longing all of us have to be loved and accepted unconditionally.

3. The need to be part of something greater than yourself.

4. The awesome suffering around the world. Your own life might be going well, but the agonies of other people might lead you to believe that only faith in God can heal the terrible divisions among people.

5. The faith and life of other people. Observing people of faith and seeing how it has changed their lives may arouse spiritual interest in a person.

6. The deep need we humans have to express gratitude. How empty it would be if we looked around at the

beauty of this world and the good things in our life and be unable to say, "Thank you, God, for all this!"

7. The assurance of knowing that human love comes from God loving us first. "This is what love is," said John, "not that we love God, but that God first loved us. Beloved, if God loved us so much, let us love one another." (1 John 4:10–11)

Each person's path to experiencing God through faith is unique. A person can say to another, "This is what helped me toward faith," but nobody can tell somebody else, "This is how it should or will happen with you."

My brother Paul was struck by a truck and killed when he was 24, a year younger than I. He had just finished his two years at Oxford as a Rhodes Scholar. His death was a terrible, terrible waste! My first reaction was anger that God had allowed this hugely gifted young man and my closest friend to be killed. Then for the first time in my life I discovered how deeply I needed God. Faith assured me that the Lord whom Paul trusted in all his life had brought him to a new level of existence, and in the midst of grief faith told me that both Paul and I were still in God's kingdom together and that Jesus's resurrection gave both of us new and eternal life. What would I have done without that faith? My anger was as fierce as ever, but God was there also.

THOMAS

The hopes of the disciples collapsed with Jesus's crucifixion. When he had been raised from death and appeared to them, they saw for themselves the astonishing miracle of the resurrection. But Thomas was not there. He desperately wanted to believe, but after the crushing blow of the crucifixion, he couldn't help but be skeptical. He had to see for himself. "Unless I see the mark of the nails in his hands, and put my finger in the mark of the nails and my hand in his side, I will not believe," he said. (John 20:25)

You and I would have said the same thing. "If Jesus is alive again, I want to see!" For a week Thomas listened to the others rejoice that Jesus was alive again. It must have been the most frustrating week of his life.

When Jesus came again, Thomas was there. "Go ahead," Jesus said to him, "touch the wounds on my hands and my side." Thomas didn't need to. The mere sight of Jesus overwhelmed him. With an awed voice he gasped, "My Lord and my God!"—a stronger statement of faith than anything said by the other disciples.

We don't see Jesus, so what does the story of Thomas mean for us? Jesus knew that he would not be appearing in bodily form anymore, so his response to Thomas was really for us:

> "Have you believed," he asked Thomas, "because you have seen me? Blessed are those who have not seen and yet have come to believe." (John 20:24–29)

That's us: We do not see Jesus, yet we can be blessed with faith and the assurance of his presence.

TWO SUGGESTIONS

The next chapter will include suggestions for the experience of God and faith. Some of the advice may not help you at all, because it won't apply to your own spiritual journey. It helps to keep two things in mind:

1. Keep searching. It is indifference, not struggle or resistance, which kills faith.
2. Faith is a gift from God. We do not "find" God. We "receive" God, and there are ways we can be receptive to this gift of experiencing God.

Note first the word "receive." That's the key. A person *receives* faith, because faith is initiated by God. God works faith in our soul, as we have seen above in Chapter 2. Once we understand that, we are freed from the urge to *do* something to achieve faith by our own efforts.

In her novel of an Indian village in British Columbia, *I Heard the Owl Call My Name*, Margaret Craven describes the Episcopalian priest Mark, who came to the shack of the dying lumberman Calamity. As Mark sat beside the cot of the dying man, Calamity says, "I ain't much of a church man, Mark. Guess you might say I'm an agnostic."

The priest replies, "There's a good bit of agnostic in all of us, Calamity. None of us knows much—only enough to trust to reach out a hand in the dark."[7]

That's what we do . . . "reach out a hand in the dark." When we reach out to God we discover that God has come to us.

---

7. Margaret Craven, *I Heard the Owl Call My Name* (Garden City, NY: Doubleday & Company, 1973), 139.

Thomas' obstacle to faith was *that he wasn't there when Jesus appeared.* He couldn't believe until he saw Jesus. Today there are places where Jesus has promised to be and where he meets us. It's not an encounter with Jesus in his bodily form as Thomas experienced, but it can be just as real.

Where are those places for us? Are they in church, in the Bible, in other people, in the needs of the world, and so on? There are several places we can start.

6

Where to Start?

> Angela, I'll always have doubts about the mysteries, as I'll always have a degree of faith. Do you know Ernest Renan's prayer? "*O God, if there is a God, save my soul, if I have a soul.*" That's me today. (Steve Randall a Methodist minister's son who had become an agnostic, speaking to his secretary, in Irving Wallace's novel, *The Word*)[1]

THE YOUNG man Steve is like the Greeks in John 12 who asked the disciples, "We want to see Jesus," or the father in Mark 9, who asked Jesus, "Lord, I believe; help my unbelief." Where should we begin in our quest to believe in and experience God?

BEING IN GOD'S PATH

We cannot summon God to us with the snap of a finger. However, God comes to us, constantly and in many ways. Faith is a gift of God, created and given by God's Spirit working within us. We cannot produce faith on our own, but we can place ourselves in God's path. Nicodemus did. He came

---

1. Irving Wallace, *The Word* (New York: Simon & Schuster, 1972), 411.

to Jesus. He was afraid, maybe embarrassed, so he sneaked out at night to meet Jesus.

We can do that too. The prophet Isaiah said, "Seek the Lord while he may be found, call upon him while he is near." (Isaiah 55:6) We can come into the path of God's Spirit. There are some places where God's presence is more clearly felt. Some of these places are obvious, some less so.

As Jesus told Nicodemus, God's Spirit blows in different ways with different people, and God meets us in different ways. (John 3) What is meaningful for you might not work at all with someone else. The best suggestion is to start someplace that is helpful for you. Here are some possibilities:

1. START WITH JESUS

Mahatma Gandhi was India's great leader in its struggle for independence. He was a Hindu, but he had a picture of Jesus on his wall. He was greatly inspired by Jesus as he formulated his political strategy of non-violence.

For anyone who has been disappointed by the church or individual Christians, a good place to begin the journey back to faith is with Jesus. After all, he is the very heart of Christianity.

Jesus was a real person, who had a very real vision for human life. It was a bold vision, quite different from the way the world usually lives. He believed that every human being had value and that our task as humans is to help the poor, the sick and the suffering. He had a loving and compassionate vision of human life, which has inspired millions of people and is behind the ideals of western civilization.

A good place to start a spiritual search would be to read the New Testament gospels—Matthew, Mark, Luke, and John. Pay close attention to the kind of person Jesus was. Then read the next books, Acts and the Epistles, and see how the incredible claim that Jesus rose from the dead transformed the lives of those who believed and followed him.

2. START WITH GOD

"In the beginning God . . . " That's how the Bible begins. God is behind it all. That's where the Christian faith begins and ends—with God. Is there a God? That's the biggest question of all.

Having lived for 15 years next to the Boundary Waters area in northern Minnesota, I have heard many people say, "When I'm in the wilderness and look up at the stars, I feel very close to God." One can't tell much *about* God through the beauty of creation, but one does get a sense that this fantastically beautiful world and universe could hardly happen by accident.

Is there more to human life than what you see around yourself? Did this universe just "become" by itself? Are we humans merely a random result of biological development over billions of years? Dr. Patricia H. Reiff, professor and department chairman of space physics and astronomy at Rice University, is a Christian. She thinks that the chances of this intricate universe happening by accident is as likely as "an explosion in a junkyard resulting in a Boeing 747 jumbo jet."[2]

A lot of people think there is no creator. A "materialist" does not believe in any kind of supernatural world apart from

2. Anderson, ibid., 59.

the "matter" we see around ourselves. It's not easy for materialists to find meaning to life or any fixed standards to live by.

On the other hand, if you believe there is "something more out there," then you are on your way to coming face-to-face with God.

"Daughters and Sons of God or Cosmic Orphans?" was a title in the newsletter of a group of Christian scientists who examine the connections between science and religious faith. Author Daniel Jungkuntz asked,

> . . . I am dust and to dust I shall return. But is all that I am just dust, a particle of nature? Or am I also created in the image of God to become a child of God?[3]

That's the alternative. We are either "daughters and sons of God" or we are "cosmic orphans."

We can't settle that question with scientific tests, philosophical arguments or test tube experiments. You can live as if there is nothing more than this materialistic world, or you can live in faith, trusting that there is more to life than what we see around us.

Do you believe there is a God, some kind of Divinity or Higher Power? If so, that's a start. But it's only a start. If you believe in a creator God, does it make sense that such a God wouldn't know human beings, the most intelligent and apparently highest form of life in creation? If you can say, "Somebody up there likes me," you have come a long, long way down the road toward believing in a personal God.

Newsweek magazine recently featured a study of American 13-year-olds. The survey revealed that two-thirds

---

3. *Works* newsletter, March-April 1995, 4.

of them said "faith was somewhat or very important in their lives." Dr. Mary Lynn Dell, who is both an adolescent psychiatrist and an Episcopal priest, said that early teen years are a time when youth develop the "ability to discern between institutional religion and an internal relationship with God." This means that "for the first time adolescents are able to take God home with them from church."[4]

Thinking about God will lead you to thinking about how we know about God, how God is revealed to us. That in turn leads us into the Bible, and in the case of Christians, to Jesus and to each other. By this process we are experiencing God.

3. START WITH THE SPIRIT

You may be a person who believes in God as someone distant who doesn't have anything to do with you. It may be helpful for you to consider God as a Spirit, the "Holy Spirit," as we say. That's the idea of the "Star War" films, where people look to a "Force" in the universe. They say to each other, "May the Force be with you." That's very similar to the greeting in Christian worship, "The Lord be with you," and the response, "And also with you."

If you believe there is a divine presence in the world today, but find it difficult to conceive of a "person" sitting someplace like heaven, start there and ask more questions: How do I discover who or what this divine presence is? How do I experience it? Ask those questions, and one way or another God will answer you.

---

4. *Newsweek*, August 8, 2005, 60–61.

4. START WITH YOUR PROBING QUESTIONS

Wrestling with God, arguing with and about God, even shaking your fist at God—all these put you very close to God. The great men and women of faith through the centuries have disputed and debated about God. Ask your questions. Find a person of faith to discuss them with. Ask the most outlandish and shocking questions you can think of. God isn't afraid of your questions, and people of faith shouldn't be either. God is the God of truth, and the more you ask the closer you can come to God.

In the Bible the wealthy man Job loses everything. His property and livestock are stolen or burned, his children are killed and his own body is afflicted with smelly sores. His exasperated wife advises him to "curse God and die!" Three friends appear and urge Job to confess whatever sins caused his misery, but Job protests that he has been faithful to God.

Job does not suffer in silence. He does not turn his back on God. He protests to God. "Let me know why you contend against me . . . Your hands fashioned and made me, and now you turn and destroy me!" (Job 20:2,8) Again and again, Job asks God why he is being tormented and why God seems to have turned away from him. "I cry to you," he says to God, "and you do not answer me. I stand, and you merely look at me!"

The message of Job is that even in the midst of his suffering, even as he argues with his friends, even when he complains, even when he wonders if God is listening to him at all—Job is always engaged with God. If Hollywood ever made a movie of Job, there would be a scene where Job shakes his fist toward heaven and angrily asks God why all this is happening!

5. START WITH PRAYER

To experience God one needs to spend time with God. That's what prayer is. Speak with God, even if you wonder if prayer does any good or if anybody listens. Most importantly, speak honestly and tell God exactly what is on your mind. We tend to pray only "nice" prayers, and when we don't feel so nice we don't talk to God at all. Why not pray like this:

> How long, God? Will you forget me forever?
> How long will you hide your face from me?
> How long must I bear pain in my soul
> and have sorrow in my heart all day long?

You would be surprised to hear a prayer like that in a church service, but it's in the Bible, Psalm 13. Those psalm writers didn't mince words with God. They spoke their minds!

This chapter began with a prayer of a man searching for faith. He quotes the honest prayer of Ernest Renan, the French religious writer of the 1800s:

> O God, if there is a God, save my soul, if I have a soul.

That's a skeptic's prayer, but it is a prayer, and any prayer is a first step in connecting a person to God.

Elie Wiesel's novel, *The Town Beyond the Wall*, is partly autobiographical about Wiesel's own return to faith after the horrors he survived in the Holocaust. In the novel Michael's faith in God has been shattered in the Nazi death camps. One day he hears a stranger's prayer that astonishes him:

> *"O God, be with me when I have need of you,*
> *but above all do not leave me when I deny you."*

The prayer is full of doubt and anguish, but it is an honest prayer. The speaker may not know what to believe about God, if anything, but by speaking to God he is engaged with God. Throughout the novel Michael constantly struggles with God. He tells a friend:

> I want to blaspheme, and I can't quite manage it. I go up against him, I shake my fist, I froth with rage, but it's still a way of telling Him that He's there, that He exists...[and] that denial itself is an offering to His grandeur. The shout becomes a prayer in spite of me.

That plain speaking with God finally leads him back to faith.[5]

In the *Newsweek* issue cited above, a New England girl reported that when she became an adolescent her prayers began to reflect her everyday concerns. "I'll pray, 'God, I don't know why I get so mad at my mom. Why am I being mean?'"[6] That's being honest with God.

I ask youth to write prayers for use in church. The first prayers they write are always full of praise, thanksgiving and requests for help. "Now," I say, "write a prayer telling God what's really going on in your life, even arguing or disagreeing with God." The prayers they wrote were different from anything they had ever prayed in their lives:

- *Dear God, my parents fight all the time. Can you do something about it?*

---

5. Elie Wiesel, *The Town Beyond the Wall* (New York: Avon Books, 1964), 49, 123.

6. *Newsweek*, ibid., 62.

- *God, I should have been chosen cheerleader, but the whole thing was unfair. Please help me get over my anger.*
- *Dear Lord, why do you allow so many children in this world to suffer?*
- *God, I'm not very popular at school. What should I do?*
- *Why don't you stop war, God? Just destroy all weapons and make them disappear.*

These are not the kind of "nice" prayers we usually hear in church, but for the first time in their lives these youth wrote prayers that were totally honest. They talked to God about the real issues in their lives. They became like Job in the Bible, arguing with God, quarreling with God, but always talking with God!

God had become part of their lives. They were "experiencing" God in faith. "Lord, help my unbelief" the boy's father said to Jesus in Mark 9. It was his prayer, straight from his heart.

6. START WITH BY ATTENDING CHURCH WORSHIP

Many people are disillusioned with the church. But faith can be found there. Most churches use prayers, songs and rituals that have been used for centuries, because they have stood the test of time and have nourished people's faith. You might feel awkward at first until you become accustomed to the service, but give it time. The wonderful music of the church, the traditions of worship, a biblical sermon that touches the issues of your life, and the faith of those around you—all these will nurture small seeds of faith within your heart that will grow. Eventually you will feel the immense power of these services that have nourished people's faith for centuries.

7. START WITH THE BIBLE

When you think about it, it is astonishing that this collection of 66 small booklets is still a best seller after twenty centuries. Obviously it has some power in it.

There are many puzzling passages in the Bible and reading it may produce more questions than answers, but God works through these words. They were written by people who have the same sorts of questions as you have, and the more one reads and studies, the more one profits from it.

8. START WITH CHRISTIAN PEOPLE

God works through people. Find Christians and ask them about their faith. David Hume, the 17th century Scottish philosopher was a thoroughgoing skeptic in religious matters. One day a friend saw him coming out of a church service where the great Methodist preacher George Whitfield had preached.

"Mr. Hume," said the friend, "I'm surprised to see you attending church. Surely you don't believe all that, do you?"

"No," answered Hume, "but Whitfield does." Hume was deeply influenced by listening to a man of intrepid faith and character like Whitfield.

Never hesitate to ask persons of faith what they believe and why. They will be more than happy to tell you.

9. START BY LOVING

Both the Old and New Testaments are very clear that faith means a new way of living. "By this everyone will know that you are my disciples," Jesus said, "if you have love for one another." Persons who serve the poor and needy are following Jesus's guidance whether they know it or not. Whatever you believe, you can realize that the world is a better place when we love others, and you can start by living a life of love. German Catholic scholar Karl Rahner coined the term "anonymous Christian" to describe people who are not professing Christians, but who live a Christian life of love. Such people cannot be far from God.

INTEREST OR DISINTEREST

The point of all these possibilities is that God creates and nurtures faith in may ways. Probing and questioning don't kill faith, but disinterest and indifference do. An honest search for faith will end in faith. God will find a way to come to you, just as surely as the waiting father rushed out to meet and embrace the prodigal son who finally came back home in Luke 15.

The tragedy is when people lose interest or become so frustrated or disappointed that they cease the quest.

THE "LEAP(S) OF FAITH"

People often use the term, "the leap of faith." Faith puts you in the company of millions of people who believe there is something more to life than what our senses tell us.

Even atheists make a "leap of faith," because they believe there is no God, an assertion one cannot prove any more than to believe that God does exist. Indeed, if we use our human reason to think about it, which makes more sense—to believe that all this vast, wonderful universe exists by mere chance, or to believe that there is an intelligent creator behind it all? It takes as radical a leap of faith to be an atheist as to believe in God!

It is better to speak of the *leaps* of faith, in the plural, because faith deepens in steps. One might begin by praying to God. It is a major step, but sooner or later one must go further and define who and what God is and what difference God makes in our lives.

Perhaps it's most accurate to say that we make "leaps" of faith every day, because faith is living and growing. Even the great saints in the Christian church were "leaping" out in faith at each step in their lives. Faith is never a finished product. You might say, "I've got it now," but what you really mean is, "I'm getting there."

Flannery O'Connor knew the struggles of faith. To one of her closest friends she wrote:

> When we get our spiritual house in order, we'll be dead. This goes on. You arrive at enough certainty to be able to make your way, but it is making it in darkness. Don't expect faith to clear things up for you. It is trust, not certainty."[7]

---

7. Ibid., 354.

7

"I Believe in God . . . the Father"

> You must picture me alone in that room night after night feeling, whenever my mind lifted even for a second from my work, the steady, unrelenting approach of Him whom I so earnestly desired not to meet. That which I greatly feared had at last come upon me. In the Trinity Term of 1929 I gave in, and admitted that God was God, and knelt and prayed: perhaps, that night, the most dejected and reluctant convert in all England. I did not then see what is now the most shining and obvious thing; the Divine humility which will accept a convert even on such terms . . . The hardness of God is kinder than the softness of humans, and His compulsion is our liberation.[1]

OXFORD PROFESSOR C. S. Lewis was an atheist, but he discovered he could not leave God alone, or, more accurately, that God would not leave him alone. In his studies, in conversations and in his deepest thoughts, God was constantly encountering him. He was not searching for faith. He was actually well satisfied with his life without God. But God was always there, beckoning him. His conversion as he

---

1. C. S. Lewis, *Surprised by Joy* (New York: Harcourt, Brace & World, Inc., 1955), 228–29.

describes it in the paragraph above was reluctant admission "that God was God," and his faith unfolded from there.

IN THE BEGINNING...

The first words in the Bible are "In the beginning God..." The first commandment is "You shall have no other gods," and the first line of the Apostles' Creed is, "I believe in God the Father..." God stands at the beginning and at the end of faith.

IS THERE A GOD?

How can I know? We have three choices:

First, I can be an *atheist*, believing there is no such thing as God—no Divinity, no "ultimate reality," no "force" above and beyond us—whatever words you might choose.

Second, I might be an *agnostic*, one who says, "I don't know, and there is no way I *can* know."

Third, I can be a *believer*. That leaves me with three further possibilities:

A. "Yes, there is a God, but that God doesn't really pay any attention to me as an individual." "Deists" believe God created the universe and set it in motion with natural laws, like a watchmaker, who produces a clock, then winds it up and lets it run by itself. This idea of God doesn't have anything to do with me personally. There are many people who may not admit it, but they live as if God were impersonal, making no difference in their lives. One might say they are "practical atheists," because they live as if there were no God.

B. Another possibility is that God is everything, and everything is part of God. This is "pan-theism," or "all-God," an old idea that has become popular again. Pantheism eliminates a God who knows us or is with us by saying that we ourselves are part of God, or even gods ourselves.

C. The third possibility is, "Yes there is a God, a God who knows me and who is deeply concerned about me." That is a far more decisive leap of faith, because once I say that, I can experience God in my life.

KNOWING GOD BY OUR REASON

How do we know God? By our own thinking and reasoning? The Apostle Paul wrote that even wicked, ungodly people can recognize God's power and wrath simply by looking at the created world:

> For what can be known about God is plain to them, because God has shown it to them. Ever since the creation of the world his eternal power and divine nature, invisible though they are, have been understood and seen through the things he has made. (Romans 1:19–20)

Medieval scholars believed that one could "prove" the existence of God by human logic. They believed that we can learn about God if we *think* logically enough. However there are problems with knowing God by our reason:

First, thinking people come up with vastly different concepts of God. Others simply dismiss the logical arguments by saying, "They might convince you, but they don't persuade me," and you're back to square one.

Second, left to our own logical thinking, we will inevitably create the kind of God we want.

Third, there is human sinfulness, which affects our minds as much other parts of our beings. How can a sinful mind be able to figure out logically and accurately who and what God is?

Nowadays, we are not so impressed or interested in such "proofs." We would say that God is neither "provable" nor "disprovable" by reasoning.

GOD REVEALED

The other way of knowing or experiencing God is to believe that God is *revealed* to us.

That is the view of the Bible. From the very beginning, God takes the initiative toward us humans. In the first books of the Old Testament God speaks directly to people—Adam, Eve, Noah, Moses, and so on. Later God speaks to people through the prophets, those individuals to whom God gives a message to deliver. "Thus speaks the Lord," they say, and they convey God's message to the listeners.

We can say a lot about God revealed as we read the Old Testament:

1. *God created everything.* That's the first verse in the Bible, and the beginning of the main statement of Christian faith, the Apostles' Creed: "I believe in God the Father almighty, creator of heaven and earth." This is truly a staggering statement of faith! Only in this century are we realizing how breathtakingly huge this universe is,

stretching out billions of light years in all directions. We believe there is a God bigger than all of this, who created it all.

2. *God gave human beings a law to live by, to enrich human life.* It is summarized in the Ten Commandments, although God also gave the Israelites many more laws governing both everyday life as well as religious observances.

3. *God is not only A God, but OUR God.* God made a covenant with Abraham, that Abraham's descendants would be God's "chosen people." (Genesis 12–17) We know nothing of a private God, because God always relates to people.

4. *God is a God not only of law, but of mercy.* God loves his people with a deep passion. Read Psalms 118 and 136, for example, with the constant repetition of the refrain, "for his steadfast love endures forever."

5. *God wants us to take care of the poor, oppressed and disadvantaged.* This is a consistent theme of the prophets in Old Testament and emphasized by Jesus in the New Testament. Prophets state that God is a God of justice, and God's justice is meant to cross national boundaries and be applied to all people. "Let justice roll down like waters and righteousness like an ever-flowing stream," wrote the prophet Amos. (Amos 5:24)

6. *Finally, God is not only* our *God, but cares for* all *people.* Most ancient peoples thought of God or the gods as their God. It was difficult for them to think of God as a God of all races and nationalities, but the prophets

made clear that God is for all peoples and nations. This is the radical message of the entire Bible.

A "MYSTIC" UNION WITH GOD?

Can you draw nearer to God by your spiritual efforts of meditation and prayer? Are some people more "spiritual" or "mystical" than others, because they achieve a closer contact to the spirit world and God? Yes, we can feel closer to God through meditation and prayer. This is not something we accomplish, but it is opening ourselves to God coming to us.

But we do not believe that there is any special class of people who are "closer" to God than others. We can all come into the presence of God in prayer, in worship and at other times. God is not available for only a privileged few, but comes to us all. Just as spending time with another person is a way to nurture and enjoy a friendship, so spending time in prayer and worship deepens our experience with God.

GOD THE FATHER

When Jesus came to earth, he referred to God as "Father." To compare God to a parent makes God more closely personal than any other word possibly could. If we have been loved and nurtured by our mother and father in our childhood, the image of God as a heavenly parent is very powerful. Even people who did not have a loving human father can well imagine how they wished for a loving father.

That's what God as "father" means. It is not a male term. We could just as well say "father and mother" or "parent." The Bible is full of motherly images of God's care, such as Jesus's lament over Jerusalem shortly before his death, "How often would I have gathered your children together as a hen gathers her brood under her wings." (Matthew 23:37)

In choosing one word for God, Christian tradition has followed Jesus and said "father." When the disciples asked Jesus to teach them to pray, he replied, "Our Father," and that became the church's most frequently used term to describe God. The very first words of the Christian creed are, "I believe in God *the Father* . . .

This is an immensely powerful statement! The God of this whole universe wants to be like a parent to you, wants you to be his child, with all your imperfections. God knows you and listens to you, just as a parent loves and listens to a child. You can trust that God is always at your side.

MORE THAN FATHER

There are two dangers in thinking of God as father.

First, our vision of God might be limited by bad examples of earthly fathers. One Sunday after a sermon about God's love, a college student asked my wife, "How can I believe God loves me if nobody has loved me?" His father disappeared shortly after his birth, and his overburdened mother sent him off to a series of foster homes, where he was considered a chronic troublemaker. In time this young man did overcome his experience of a bad father by realizing that the Bible shows us a loving heavenly parent.

Second, God is "my" father, but faith is more than a private thing between God and me. The one prayer Jesus taught us, the "Lord's Prayer," begins "Our Father," not "My Father."

The words "I" or "me" are not in the Lord's Prayer at all. Faith connects me with people all over the world.

GOD . . . CREATOR OF HEAVEN AND EARTH

The Apostles' Creed begins with the intimate, family term "father," but immediately expands the idea of God into cosmic dimensions, " . . . almighty, creator of heaven and earth." The first two short chapters in the Bible boldly assert that all creation comes from God.

If a person believes this, a whole series of implications follow. Any possibility of a cozy religion between just God and me is wiped away. God is my heavenly father and mother, but God is also creator of the whole universe! God is father and mother to all human beings. I am not an only child—I have a vast array of brothers and sisters, all over this world! Jim Wallis, founder and editor of *Sojourners* magazine, often says, "God is personal, but not private." In experiencing God we also experience a feeling that we are part of vast human family.

One of the great blessings of the world, and one of its greatest curses, is "tribalism." A person needs to belong to somebody. Children need the security of a family and a larger circle of relatives and friends, as well as a sense of belonging to a community and finally to a nation. We get our very identity from the "tribes" we belong to.

However, if we identify totally with our "tribe," it is an easy step to mistreat other "tribes." Look around at the misery of the world. How often one group of people is opposed to another group of people, and the conflict erupts into violence and killing. That's the disastrous side of "tribalism." Human history is full of it, and every day newspapers carry stories of suffering and heartache from tribalism run rampant.

What happens to tribalism when people believe in a creator God? Of course we belong to our own "tribes"—families, communities and nations—but we know that we also belong to the whole human race, because God is creator and father, the heavenly parent of us all!

GOD'S PEOPLE, THE ENVIRONMENTALISTS

Ecology and the environment have become front-page news. Air pollution, the thinning of the ozone layer, global warming, land erosion, filth in our rivers and lakes, nuclear waste, the loss of rainforests, the destruction of farm land, the shrinking amount of natural resources—all these topics are part of the news every day.

In the Bible God says to Adam and Eve, " . . . fill the earth and subdue it, and have dominion over the fish of the sea and over the birds of the air and over every living thing that moves upon the earth." (Genesis 1:28) Some people blame our ecological problems on Christians who think that God's instructions give us permission to do anything we want to the environment. That is not what the Bible means. "Subdue" and "have dominion" imply responsibility. "Have dominion over" means "take care of" the world.

Rulers have dominion over their subjects. Bad rulers might exploit and mistreat their subjects, but good rulers know that they are responsible for the well being of their people.

Once we believe that the world is God's creation we see our role as caretakers of God's world. We recognize nature as a gift of God to be treasured and tended, not to be exploited and polluted.

THE GOD WE KNOW

How do we know about God? The astonishing claim of Christianity is that we believe God came to earth. We believe that Jesus of Nazareth is God's Son, God in human form, God's most real and concrete revelation. No longer do we have to speculate about a distant God. Jesus is God on a human level, with us.

8

"I Believe in God . . . the Son"

> I decided it was now or never; I wanted to get to the truth of the matter. So I prayed, quite honestly, "Jesus, I don't know if you even exist, but I'll try you out. I'll give you control of my life and you reveal yourself to me." . . . Millions of people have claimed that Jesus has revealed himself to them in response to actions of honest surrender that are analogous to my own experience.[1]

HOW DO WE KNOW GOD?

THE CENTRAL truth of Christianity is a *person*, Jesus of Nazareth. We believe Jesus was the "Messiah," the person whom God promised to send. Jesus taught his followers many things, but in the end it was *he* they believed in, not just his teachings. "I am the way, and the truth, and the life," he told them. (John 14:6)

The famous missionary E. Stanley Jones told about a missionary who became lost in the African jungle. He wandered around, without finding any familiar landmarks. At last he came upon a small settlement of native huts and asked if

---

1. John Suppe, Professor of Geosciences at Princeton University, "Ordinary Memoir," *Professors Who Believe*, ibid., 71–72.

someone could show him the way. "Follow me," one of the natives said, and set off. As they hacked their way through the jungle, the missionary became worried because they didn't seem to be on any path. "Are you sure this is the way?" he asked. "Where is the path?" The native turned and answered, "Bwana, in this place there is no path. *I* am the path."

That's what Jesus is for us—the path to true and abundant life. He doesn't just *show* us the way, he *is* the way. God did not just send the Ten Commandments, creeds, or a list of dogmas to believe in. God came to earth. In Jesus we meet God person-to-person.

A mother was putting her little girl to bed. When the light was turned off, the girl was afraid and asked, "Mother, am I going to be left all alone in the dark?" Her mother replied, "Yes, but you have God with you all the time."

"I know that God is with me all the time," the child answered, "but I want somebody who has a face."

That's Jesus—God with a human face, God who has lived on earth as one of us and who has promised to be with us each day. Jesus is our path though whom we are restored to God, and our experience of Jesus in our lives is our experience of God. Even non-Christians recognize Jesus as one of the most remarkable and influential persons who ever lived. For Christians he is that, but much, much more. He is the Son of God, our Savior, "Immanuel," a Hebrew word meaning "God with us"!

JESUS—THE HEART OF FAITH

More books have been written about Jesus than about any other person in history. Yet we have only scant details of his life. We don't even know the exact date of his birth or his death. We have four short books about Jesus—Matthew, Mark, Luke and John—but they were written as testimonies, not as biographies in today's sense.

Despite our lack of knowledge about the details of his life, one fact emerges: Jesus was an astonishing and unique human being! A description of this "One Solitary Life" written by an unknown author is often quoted:

> He was born in an obscure village, the child of a peasant woman. He grew up in another village. He worked in a carpenter shop until he was 30, and then for three years was an itinerant preacher. He never wrote a book. He never held office. He never owned a home. He never traveled 200 miles from the place where he was born. He never did one of the things that usually accompany greatness. He had no credentials but himself.
>
> Although he walked the land over, curing the sick, giving sight to the blind, healing the lame and raising people from the dead, the established religious leaders turned against him. His friends ran away. He was turned over to enemies. He went through the mockery of a trial. He was spat upon, flogged and ridiculed. He was nailed to a cross between two thieves. While he was dying, the executioners gambled for the only piece of property he had on earth, and that was his robe. When he was dead, he was laid in a borrowed grave through the pity of a friend.
>
> Nineteen centuries have come and gone, and today he is the central figure of the human race and a leader of the column of progress.

> All the armies that ever marched, and all the navies that were ever built, and all the parliaments that ever sat, and all the kings that ever reigned, put together, have not affected the lives of people upon this earth as has that *One Solitary Life*.

By any measure Jesus was an amazing human being. Little did the Roman governor of Jerusalem, Pontius Pilate, realize what truth he spoke when he brought Jesus before the angry, snarling crowd and said, "Here is the man!" (John 19:1–5) He knew Jesus was innocent and no doubt admired his courage. Yet he condemned him to death to avoid the mob's disapproval. We could translate Pilate's statement as, "Now here is a *real* man!" He was correct, but had no idea how that phrase would ring true down through the ages. Pontius Pilate would have been totally forgotten by history, but he is now a household name known around the world whenever a Christian creed is spoken.

When the late English scholar J.B. Phillips translated the New Testament into modern English, he was struck anew by the person of Jesus—a man of singular vitality, courage and integrity. Phillips then wrote another book, describing how the portrait of Jesus in these New Testament books does indeed have the "ring of truth":

> I was not at all prepared for the *unconventional* man revealed in these terse Gospels. No one could possibly have invented such a person: this was no puppet-hero built out of the imaginations of adoring admirers. "This man Jesus" so briefly described, rang true, sometimes alarmingly true. I began to see now why the religious Establishment of those

days wanted to get rid of him at all costs. He was sudden death to pride, pomposity and pretense.[2]

Read the four gospels and you cannot escape being captured by the personality of Jesus. He combines all the best about human life—strong yet gentle, compassionate yet tough-minded, capable of weeping and anger, constantly among people yet needing to be alone at times, loving sinful people without approving of their sin, plain looking yet obviously a magnetic personality, simple life-style yet able to associate with the wealthy and powerful. One does not have to be a Christian to realize that Jesus of Nazareth was an absolutely unique human being in all history!

WORLDLY, UN-WORLDLY, OR OTHER-WORLDLY?

Many religions have a strong impulse to escape from the world because of its sin and cruelty. They are "unworldly"—not interested in this earthly life—or they are "other-worldly"—focusing on the hopes for the world to come. Common stereotypes of these kinds of religion are a man meditating by himself before a remote cave or a robed monk who has given up all worldly goods and now begs for food. Some people use religion to withdraw from everyday life.

This is not true of Christianity. Quite the opposite! Someone once observed, "Christianity is the *most worldly* of all religions." We not only believe that God created the world, but also that God is passionately interested in the welfare of this world and its people. The first Bible verse children mem-

2. J. B. Phillips, *Ring of Truth* (London: Hodder & Stoughton, Ltd., 1967), 87.

orize is usually John 3:16: "For God so loved the world that he gave his only Son . . . " That's where it all starts: God *loves* this world! God loves the world through Jesus.

Jesus immersed himself in the life of this world. He waded into the swirl of human life to heal, feed and restore those in need. He was constantly surrounded by people who were poor, sick, suffering, hungry and dying. He loved this world and the people in it with all his heart. Indeed, he gave his life for them all.

SALVATION—FROM WHAT?

Why did Jesus come to earth? Why did God send his Son to be born as a human being and to die as a common criminal?

The short answer is sin. The drama began in the creation story, when Adam and Eve ate the fruit of the tree that God had forbidden. Adam and Eve followed their own desires rather than the will of God. God is the one who decides what is good and evil, and when human beings ignore God's way and indulge their own desires, a Pandora's box is opened and all sorts of tragic and ugly consequences pour out.

The story about Adam and Eve disobeying God is really the story about you and me, every human being. The basic sin of Adam and Eve is reflected in all of us.

The source of sin is self-centeredness and pride. This pride is not the healthy self-esteem which every person needs, but a kind of pride which lifts oneself up at the expense of others. Think about it: All the evil and the troubles in the world between human beings stem from human self-centeredness over against the well being of others. It is no wonder that the second sin recorded in the Bible is murder. Cain was angry that his brother Abel's sacrifice was more acceptable. Cain's pride was wounded, and he struck to kill.

List the problems among people in the world today, and you can trace each one back to this fundamental sin of self-centeredness—murder, stealing, abuse, political corruption, economic exploitation, meanness, adultery, disregard for the poor, for minority people, or for anybody different from me, etc.

Look through any newspaper. Mark in yellow those headlines that tell how somebody or some group did something wrong against others because they want things their way. You'll end up with yellow blotches on every page!

This sinfulness has resulted in separation on four levels:

A. Separation from God. Having broken God's laws, humans instinctively fear God. Over the centuries religions have devised all kinds of ways to appease an angry God or gods, sometimes by setting up and worshiping idols.

B. Separation from other people. Human life is full of anger, misunderstanding, loneliness, and resentment. Often we are meanest to those closest to us.

C. Separation from creation. In our desire to get what we want, we have exploited, littered and polluted our environment. Human beings are by far the most destructive and disruptive element of nature.

D. Separation from our true self. Many human beings have no idea of a meaning or purpose in their lives and feel lonely or unfulfilled.

Every one of us has experienced those kinds of separations.

SALVATION—FOR WHAT?

How will God put all this back together again? Merely laying down the law for humans didn't work. God did that with Moses and the Ten Commandments, but people continued to disobey. Furthermore, the law reinforces the fear we have of God, because then we know for sure we've fallen short.

God needed to show us concretely what human life was intended to be like at its very best. What better way than to become a human being and live that kind of life?

That human being was Jesus. His life was quite the opposite of a self-centered life. He lived for other people. He healed the sick, fed the hungry, encouraged the downtrodden, and reconciled those who had separated themselves from others. He lived a life of love for others, the opposite of a sinful life.

Living as a human, Jesus suffered the consequences of sin. Religious and political leaders put him to death to protect their own interests, that is, in their self-centeredness. He became a sacrifice, taking upon himself the result and punishment of sin—for us.

Yet in his hour of terrible agony on the cross, Jesus spoke words of forgiveness, "Father, forgive them, for they don't know what they're doing." God gave himself, his Son on earth, to forgive and save us.

The central miracle of Christianity is that God raised Jesus from the dead. The resurrection is the towering message of the Christian faith: In the resurrection Jesus conquered the very forces of death and evil. Even more, he has conquered death for his followers too and brings us into eternal life with him.

The New Testament makes that very clear. Paul wrote to the Romans,

> Therefore we have been buried with him by baptism into death, so that just as Christ was raised from the dead by the glory of the Father, so we too might walk in newness of life. For if we have been united with him in a death like his, we will certainly be united with him in a resurrection like his. (Romans 6:4–5)

We experience this new life of resurrection in different ways.

REDEEMED AND RESTORED

Salvation is more than just waiting for heaven. Jesus brings healing to all areas of sin and brokenness in our lives. What are the troubling issues for you? What prevents your life from fullness and joy?

"Godspell" is a dramatic portrayal of Jesus's life in popular music. When the prodigal son returns home after wasting his father's inheritance, he and the chorus sing "We Beseech Thee." The chorus names problems we humans face, and the son answers how Jesus meets these situations:

> Sick!—We come to Thee for cure,
> Guilty!—We seek Thy mercy sure,
> Evil!—We long to be made pure,
> Blind!—We pray that we may see,
> Bound!—We pray to be made free,
> Strained!—We pray for sanctity,
> We beseech Thee, hear us! . . .

You cannot put Jesus in a pigeon-hole and say, "*This one thing* is what Jesus came to do." His life, death and resurrection accomplished many things. Jesus confronted and dealt with the whole spectrum of human needs.

- He was a sacrifice for sin, but one cannot limit his whole ministry to his death on the cross.
- He was an example for living, but he was more than an exalted moral teacher.
- He was an advocate for the poor, but he was more than a social reformer.
- He is "my personal savior," but he came to establish a new people, a new fellowship of believers, a community of people.
- His resurrection conquered the power of death and opened eternity for us, but his life shows us what true life on this earth is intended to be.
- He lived 2000 years ago, yet he lives among his people now and promises to be with always.
- He was a deeply spiritual man, yet he cared passionately about everyday concerns—how we spend money, good health, how we treat each other, and so on.

In today's language Jesus is "multi-dimensional." Whoever you are, and whatever your situation in life is, Jesus meets you with the grand and wonderful good news of God's redemption! The Bible uses many words to describe the salvation Jesus brings: forgiveness, reconciliation, acceptance, joy, meaning, restoration, purpose, *shalom*, eternal life, and so on. It's all there, from Jesus!

TAKE HIM SERIOUSLY!

Jesus wants followers, disciples. His intent is to remake those who believe in him. The one thing he does *not* want is to leave us unchanged. The Apostle Paul found that out, when Jesus appeared to him and totally changed his entire life. "So if anyone is in Christ," Paul wrote of his experience, "there is a new creation: everything old has passed away; see, everything has become new!" (2 Corinthians 5:17)

When C. S. Lewis wrote about his faith he used pointed language about taking Jesus seriously:

> I am trying here to prevent anyone saying the really foolish thing that people often say about Him: "I'm ready to accept Jesus as a great moral teacher, but I don't accept His claim to be God." That is the one thing we must not say. A man who was merely a man and said the sort of things Jesus said would not be a great moral teacher. He would either be a lunatic—on a level with the man who says he is a poached egg—or else he would be the Devil of Hell. You must make your choice. Either this man was, and is, the Son of God: or else a madman or something worse. You can shut Him up for a fool, you can spit at Him and kill Him as a demon; or you can fall at His feet and call Him Lord and God. But let us not come with any patronizing nonsense about His being a great human teacher. He has not left that open to us. He did not intend to.[3]

---

3. C. S. Lewis, *Mere Christianity* (New York: Macmillan Publishing Co., 1943), 55–56.

Geoffrey Studdert-Kennedy was a popular British military chaplain in World War One. After the war he became a champion for social justice, convinced that faith in Jesus compelled us to work for disadvantaged people. He described the tragedy of not taking Jesus seriously in a poem, titled "Indifference":

> When Jesus came to Golgatha they hanged Him on a tree,
> They drove great nails through hands and feet, and made a Calvary;
> They crowned Him with a crown of thorns, red were His wounds and deep,
> For those were crude and cruel days, and human flesh was cheap.
> When Jesus came to Birmingham, they simply passed Him by,
> They never hurt a hair of Him, they only let Him die;
> For men had grown more tender, and they would not give Him pain,
> They only just passed down the street, and left Him in the rain.
> Still Jesus cried, "Forgive them, for they know not what they do,"
> And still it rained the winter rain that drenched Him through and through;
> The crowds went home and left the streets without a soul to see,
> And Jesus crouched against a wall and cried for Calvary.[4]

---

4. G. A. Studdert Kennedy, *Masterpieces of Religious Verse* (Grand Rapids, MI: Baker Book House, 1948, 1978 edition), 195.

9

"I Believe in God . . . the Holy Spirit"

> "I'll give you a silver coin if you can tell me where God is," said a skeptic to his friend.
> "And I'll give you a gold coin if you can tell me where God isn't," replied the friend.

THE FRIEND was right. God is everywhere. That brings us to the Holy Spirit. If we stopped with God the Father and God the Son, we might end up believing that God created us and saved us, then left us to our own devices.

That is the answer of the 1977 film "Oh, God," where God comes to earth in the form of George Burns. It's a very funny film, filled with interesting insights, but the ending is far different than the message of the Bible. When George Burns as God leaves, he describes his work to Jerry, the young grocery clerk played by John Denver:

> "You drop a few seeds and you move on. The seeds are good, they take root. I gave you good seeds—the best. I'd better be going."
> Jerry asks, "Aren't you coming back?"
> God answers, "No."
> "Ever?"
> "When 'ever' comes. We'll see."

> Jerry asks, "Sometimes . . . now and then . . . couldn't we just talk."
>
> George Burns smiles, pats Jerry on the cheek, and says, "I'll tell you what. You talk. I'll listen." Then he disappears. Jerry knows he'll never see or hear from him again.

That's a God without the Holy Spirit . . . an absentee God. It's the watchmaker God. He made a wonderfully intricate watch, gets it going and then leaves it to run. That kind of God gave us "good seeds," and now leaves us to do the best we can with them.

The Christian God is different. "I believe in the Holy Spirit" is the confident trust that we experience God because God's Spirit is around us and within us.

"I NEED THY PRESENCE . . . "

Henry Francis Lyte was born in Scotland about two hundred years ago and became the pastor of a small seaside parish in Lower Brixham, England. Failing health forced him to resign, and his friends urged him not even to preach on his last Sunday in the parish. He replied, "It is better to *wear* out than to *rust* out!" He preached that day, and later in the evening he wrote a hymn which would make him famous. The next week he left England for the sunnier weather of Italy, but died before reaching his destination.

In a world which hungers for the assurance of God's presence with us, Henry Lyte's hymn "Abide with Me" has become a favorite everywhere with its firm confidence:

> I need thy presence every passing hour;
> What but thy grace can foil the tempter's power?

> Who but thyself my guide and stay can be?
> Through cloud and sunshine, O abide with me!

It was written as comfort at the time of death, but the words are meant for all of life.

St. Patrick was the "Apostle to the Irish," and patron saint of Ireland. He first came to Ireland as a slave, having been captured by raiders at age 16. Six years later he escaped and hoped he would never see Ireland again. God had other plans. Patrick had a vision that he would return and evangelize the island. He became a priest and went to Ireland as assistant to the bishop, whom he succeeded in A.D. 432. His work as a missionary was far more dangerous than his six years in slavery, because the Druids and other powerful forces opposed him. Gradually the faith he brought spread and Christianity became the faith of the country.

Patrick composed a prayer, which he called his "Breastplate," a prayer for God's protection and presence. One of the verses expresses all the ways God is with him:

> I arise today through
> God's strength to pilot me,
> God's might to uphold me,
> God's wisdom to guide me,
> God's eye to look before me,
> God's ear to hear me,
> God's word to speak for me,
> God's hand to guard me,
> God's way to lie before me,
> God's shield to protect me,
> God's host to save me
> From snares of devils,
> From temptations of vices,

> From every one who shall wish me ill,
> Far and near,
> Alone and in multitude!

Is there any time or circumstance or any aspect of life where God is absent from us? Patrick's answer is a resounding "No!" His "breastplate" prayer can be ours too.

A "FEELING"

Can we "feel" God's presence? Sometimes. You might have a sense of God's presence at a worship service, or listening to beautiful music. People have that kind of feeling at different times. I have that feeling looking at a beautiful scene in nature. Certain pieces of music trigger that feeling for me. When I hear a choir sing "O God, Our Help in Ages Past" or "Praise to the Lord, the Almighty," or Bach's organ chorale "Jesu Joy of Man's Desiring," I feel as I'm in God's very presence. Other people have that feeling with other music.

However, some people may not "feel" much at all. What's most important is the *faith* that God's Spirit is indeed with us, even when you don't "feel" anything. That's why faith in God and the experience of God go hand-in-hand.

A friend of mine went through a period of dark depression. "I can't even pray to God, anymore," he said, "because I feel as if God is a million miles away from me. My prayers don't even seem to get beyond the ceiling of the room."

My response was, "God has promised to be with you, and you can trust that even if you don't feel anything. God will not let you go, no matter what you feel!" Faith can pull us through the hard times in our lives, even when our feelings seem empty.

BACK TO THE BASICS

A 9th grader came to my office one spring day a week before confirmation.

> "I don't think I can be confirmed," she said.
>
> "Why not," I asked.
>
> "Because I don't think I believe all the things I'm supposed to believe for confirmation."
>
> "Like what?"
>
> "Well, for instance, I don't really understand the Trinity, especially where it gets really complicated in the Creed—'God from God, Light from Light, true God from true God, begotten, not made, of one being with the Father'—and so on."
>
> "Scholars have discussed the Trinity for centuries," I said. "Maybe nobody can 'understand' it, because all our descriptions are limited by our human brains and language. God is greater than all that. But terms like the 'Trinity' help us understand what God is like and what God is doing. That's why we use them."

We talked about other items as well, questions she had about the Bible and beliefs that the church held.

> Her question still hung in the air: "Should I be confirmed?"
>
> Finally I said, "Do you believe there is a God, that is, that there is Someone out there greater than yourself, who is somehow behind all creation?"
>
> "Sure," she said. "I've always believed that."

"And what do you think about Jesus?" I asked.

"I like him a lot," she answered.

"Do you think God sent him, that he's close to God in some way more than we are?" I asked.

"Yes, that seems pretty clear from reading the Bible."

"Do you believe in some way he saved us by being crucified and raised again and made it possible for us to be restored and united back to God? When you see Jesus' vision for human life, of love and concern for all people, is that how you want to pattern your life too?"

"Sure," she said. "I think he lived the perfect human life and that he saved us."

"Do you believe that God is still present in people's lives, like right here with you and me now?"

"Yes," she said, "I think God is always with me."

"Then you believe enough to be confirmed," I said. "You have just affirmed the heart of the Christian faith. There's a lot of doctrine, history and biblical knowledge you don't know yet, but you have the essentials—God the Father, Son and Holy Spirit. I'm sure you will continue to grow in faith, understanding and living, but from what you have told me now you should be confirmed."

And so she was, that next Sunday.

THE TRINITY

The Bible is very clear that there is one God. For both Jews and Christians, Deuteronomy 6:4 is a cornerstone of faith: "Hear, O Israel: The Lord our God is one God."

Christians believe God is the creator. We also believe Jesus is God in human form. And we also believe that God in Spirit is everywhere present. In order to put those three statements together without thinking of three Gods, the church used the term "Trinity," or "tri-une" God. To omit one of the three would be to neglect some part of God's presence and activity with us.

We often use analogies to explain the Trinity, this "three-in-one" God. According to legend, when Patrick went as a missionary to Ireland, the pagan Irish were confused about the Trinity. Patrick bent down, picked a three-leafed clover and asked, "Is this three leaves or one?" It is obviously one leaf, but there are three parts to it. Ever since that time the three-leafed shamrock has been a much loved symbol for the Irish people.

When I was a boy one of my teachers told us to imagine a pie, cut into three pieces. Is it one pie or three? It was one pie. The three pieces were of the same "stuff," but each was unique, slightly different than the others.

Neither of these analogies is perfect, but they do help understand the mystery of the Trinity. Faith in the Trinity assures us that God has created us, loves us, saves us, walks beside us each day, and at our deathbed will bring us into eternal life. We're not alone anymore, ever. God is with us—Father, Son, and Holy Spirit.

LIFE IN THREE DIMENSIONS

In the 1972 film "Save the Tiger," Jack Lemmon won an Oscar for his portrayal of businessman Harry Stoner. In one scene he picks up a young woman hitchhiking. To pass the time they play a game where they take turns naming a person for the other to identify. Harry names Mo Purtill, Henry Wallace, Herman Göring, Fred Allen and Cookie Lavagetto. The girl doesn't know any of them. She names the Beatles, Rolling Stones, Grateful Dead and New Riders of the Purple Sage. He can't identify any of them.

Harry realizes that the two of them live in different worlds. "She doesn't have a past," he observes, "and I don't have a present."

Past history is often not a popular subject in schools. For the "Now Generation" what matters is today.

At the other end of time, many people don't like to think about the future. In some respects it looks pretty bleak. It seems harder to get a good job now than in the past. Some social problems are worse now than in the past. It's easy to be pessimistic.

Faith in God stretches out the horizons of our lives more than we could ever imagine.

1. Past. Through faith in God the Father I am connected with the whole creation. I am part of the human family that stretches back to Adam and Eve, including all the great saints of the church. Abraham is my father in faith, because God made a covenant with him, and I'm included in that promise.

2. Present. Because God's Holy Spirit is always with me, I live in the constant presence of God. The last thing Jesus spoke to his disciples before leaving them and ascending to heaven was the promise of his presence: "And lo, I am with you always, to the close of the age." (Matthew 28:20) We don't have to split hairs about which "part" of God is with us. The Bible speaks of the presence of God, Jesus, and the Spirit interchangeably.

3. Future. Because Jesus conquered the forces of death by his resurrection, my future has broken through the barrier of my physical death, and I look forward to an endless future in eternity.

THE HOLY SPIRIT—GOD HERE AND NOW

One of my favorite towns in Europe is Rovinj, Croatia, on the Adriatic Sea. The old part of town is on a hill next to the sea, with narrow streets winding up to the church on the top of the hill. The whitewashed stone buildings are jammed together like a huge rabbit warren. Narrow stairways lead off the street up into the second and third stories. There are more people living on that small hill than in a sprawling American town, where each house is an isolated island in a sea of green lawns.

Even if you're single in Rovinj, you are never alone. People live all around you, and the moment you step outside you are among friends and neighbors.

How different from America, where loneliness is one of today's major social problems! People often live separated from their families. Many people don't even know their own neighbors. A person can live in a crowded apartment complex and be terribly lonely, because everybody is too busy with their own lives to get together.

Belief in the Holy Spirit is the belief that God's Spirit is always with us. Anybody feeling lonely should think of Psalm 139, a wonderful affirmation that even when we feel totally abandoned, God is with us:

> O LORD, you have searched me and known me.
> You know when I sit down and when I rise up;
> you discern my thoughts from far away ...
> Where can I go from your spirit?
> Or where can I flee from your presence?
> If I ascend to heaven, you are there;
> if I make my bed in Sheol, you are there.
> If I take the wings of the morning
> and settle at the farthest limits of the sea,
> even there your hand shall lead me,
> and your right hand shall hold me fast ...

EVERYDAY PRESENCE

When we think of God's presence, we usually think of religious people, perhaps those who pray or meditate a lot. Sometimes we become too busy with everyday affairs to think much about God, to say nothing of sensing God's presence with us.

Nicholas Herman was born in 1611 in Lorraine, France. At age 18 he became a Christian and joined the army. In his mid-50s he entered a Carmelite Monastery in Paris and took Lawrence as his new name. He lacked the education to become a priest so he was assigned to ordinary kitchen duty and later on to the shoe repair shop. Over the years people realized that he lived with a sense of God's presence not only during worship but also in the kitchen midst the clanging and clattering of pots and pans. After he died in 1691 his letters were made public with the title *The Practice of the Presence of God*, which soon became a classic of religious literature. In his first letter the dish-washing monk wrote,

> It is not necessary to be always in church to be with God. We can make a private chapel of our heart where we can retire from time to time to commune with Him—peacefully, humbly, lovingly. Everone is capable of these intimate conversations with God, some more, some less. He knows what we can do. Let us begin—perhaps He is only waiting for a single generous resolution from us.[1]

God is with you every minute of every day, waking or sleeping. That's God's promise to you. While the other monks were in the chapel experiencing God through the beauty of their singing and the art around them, Brother Lawrence was equally confident of God's presence as he bent over the dirty pots in the sink.

If we spoke only of God the Father and God the Son, it might be tempting to limit God to the past and to the future. Add the Holy Spirit, and we are assured of God's vibrant and strong presence in our lives—every day!

---

1. Brother Lawrence, *The Practice of the Presence of God* (Garden City NY: Doubleday & Co.., Image Books, 1977), 65.

10

How Then Shall We Live?

"Remember who you are—the son of a King."
(From "The Lion King," a 1994 Walt Disney film)

"SON AND DAUGHTERS OF THE KING"

In the film "The Lion King" a careless lion cub causes the death of his lion-king father. The shamed and grief-stricken cub runs away and fritters his days away. In his absence the hyenas take over and ruin the lions' territory. One day the young lion's exile is interrupted by a vision of his father, who summons his son back to his place as the new lion king in order to restore the kingdom. The old lion-king tells his son to "Remember who you are—the son of a king. Remember who you are."

To experience God means to see ourselves and our lives in a whole new way. Our lives matter. They matter a lot, because they matter to God.

Who are we as human beings? The old lion's advice is for us too. While we are on earth, where we cannot see the grand kingdom of God, we are summoned to remember who we are—sons and daughters of the king! We are sons and daughters of the King of all creation! Even the most ordinary lives can be full of joy and meaning when we realize who we are!

How shall we live? That depends on what you think you are as a human being, and that leads back to some more basic questions:

- What's human life all about? That leads back to a really basic question:
- What's your purpose in life? And that in turns leads to the deepest question:
- Who are *you*?

A BIOLOGICAL WONDER

Who are you? The first and obvious answer is: we are mammals on this planet. You could say, "That's all we are—really smart animals!" If that's my answer, then I will live my life as a biological being with the essentials of physical life—food, housing, clothes, security and comfort.

I'll want other things too. If I want power and authority, I'll seek a position of importance and enjoy being boss. If it's physical pleasure I want, then I'll want gourmet food and an attractive companion. If it's companionship that makes me happy, I'll hope for a large family and circle of friends. If I enjoy mental stimulation, then reading and conversation will be important for me.

Of course we are part of this biological world, and live as biological beings. A person could stop searching for any further meaning, and settle for life on a purely pleasurable level. Without God in the picture what would be our standard of actions? If there is no God the only sense of right and wrong might be whatever I wish to do and could get away with. Who's to say I shouldn't do exactly what I want?

A CONSCIENCE

Take God out of the picture. What is a human being then? How will we live? By what standards? By whose standards?

We know that there is more to a human being than our biological makeup. We have instincts and intelligence. By instinct we protect ourselves, our children and loved ones. Our sexual drives guarantee reproduction. We are capable of courage, even selfless and sacrificial actions. Animals too have instincts and some intelligence, and some have done heroic deeds of rescue.

But there is something more with us humans. We are the one creature in nature with a conscience.

In the process of becoming a Christian, C. S. Lewis observed that every human being and every human society has a sense of right and wrong or a set of laws which cannot be explained by biological development, instinct or habit. This sense of law, or conscience, had to come *from* someplace or someone.

> It begins to look as if we shall have to admit that there is more than one kind of reality, that, in this particular case, there is something above and beyond the ordinary facts of man's behavior."[1]

That idea was for C. S. Lewis the first step in his becoming a Christian. He realized that the idea of God as the creator of the "moral law" is "not yet within a hundred miles of the

---

1. C. S. Lewis, *Mere Christianity*, ibid., 30.

God of Christian theology",[2] but for him this insight was the breakthrough to believe there is a God. The existence of the human conscience opened his vision to something beyond this visible world.

WHO ARE YOU? WHAT IS A HUMAN BEING?

We humans are intended to be connected to the whole universe. Our ultimate human destiny is to experience and live with God.

John Gillespie Magee, a 19-year-old American volunteer pilot with the Royal Canadian Air Force, was killed in action on December 11, 1941. Shortly before he died, he wrote "High Flight," a poem well-known by pilots. It expresses his thrill of flying and finally our destiny with God:

> Oh, I have slipped the surly bonds of earth,
> And danced the skies on laughter-silvered wings
> Sunward I've climbed and joined the tumbling mirth
> Of sun-split clouds—and done a hundred things
> You have not dreamed of...
> Up, up the long, delirious, burning blue
> I've topped the wind-swept heights with easy grace,
> Where never lark, or even eagle, flew;
> And, while with silent, lifting mind I've trod
> The high untrespassed sanctity of space,
> Put out my hand, and touched the face of God.[3]

---

2. Ibid., 34.

3. John Gillespie Magee, "High Flight," *On the Wing: American Poems of Air and Space Flight* (Iowa City IA: University of Iowa Press, 2005), 46.

That's what we humans are meant to do in faith—slip the surly bonds of earth and touch the very face of God.

A story is told of a farmer who once found an abandoned egg and put it under a hen in the chicken coop. When it hatched, he discovered it was a baby eagle. The little eaglet followed the other chickens, walked about the chicken yard and picked up bits of grain for food. As the eagle grew, it did not realize that it was different from the other chickens. Finally the farmer decided it was time for the eagle to fly away and live like an eagle. Every time he tossed it into the air, the eagle fluttered back to the ground and joined the other chickens pecking for grain.

One day the eagle heard the screech of another eagle soaring in the sky, and the piercing cry stirred something deep within. The eagle looked up at the sky, ruffled its wings with excitement, and then with a screech of its own took off into the sky. It had become what it was intended to be and would never again return to the chicken yard.

Human beings are meant to be eagles, not chickens. A lot of people don't realize that. They spend their lives pecking around for food in the farmyard and never soar through the sky on the rising air currents. We get side-tracked and lose track of who we are.

TRAVELLING WITH A PASSPORT

If you are in a foreign country, you show who you are by showing your passport. You might be in London, Calcutta, Hong Kong, Istanbul or Nairobi, but the passport in your backpack shows who you actually are.

We Christians are like foreign travelers with passports in our pockets. Our passport is the Christian faith. It identifies us as part of a worldwide family no matter where we go, but also identifies us as a citizen of God's kingdom, a realm that goes beyond even this earth.

The first time I went behind the Iron Curtain was during the coldest of the Cold War years. The Berlin Wall had just been erected, and the armies on both sides of the line were on full alert. I was to attend a meeting in Czechoslovakia. At the Czech border I was ordered out of my car by guards carrying machine guns and summoned into the customs office. There I was searched and interrogated by suspicious and angry officials.

Finally I was allowed to continue my trip, and I arrived in Prague feeling very nervous in this hostile and alien place. However, when I went to church on Sunday morning, I was surrounded by Christians. I had never met any of them before, but I felt a deeply moving bond with these total strangers. It was a totally unexpected and amazing feeling! At that moment I felt as close to them as if they were biological sisters and brothers. We shared a faith, and we were part of a kingdom which was far greater than any government on earth. The government had the guns and artillery, but we had Jesus' promise that no power of evil in the world could prevail against God's people!

My wife was born in Hungary and came to the USA as a young girl with her family. Still fluent in the Hungarian language, she was an American delegate to the 1984 Lutheran World Federation assembly in Budapest. We were examined by hostile guards at the border, then checked into a hotel where police were stationed around the clock at every entrance. Our rooms were probably bugged, so we dared not speak openly. We felt like outsiders in an enemy camp. But when the assembly began we entered a huge arena and were thrilled as hundreds of gallant Hungarian Christians were singing, "A Mighty Fortress" to welcome fellow Christians from around the world. Once again we were with "our people."

You don't have to go to another country to experience this. Any time you go into a church, even if you don't know anybody there, you are with brothers and sisters in faith.

THE "HAPPINESS MACHINE"

Sometimes we dream of being rich, famous, or powerful. We read magazines and envy those celebrities who live their millionaire lives. We love to speculate "if only"—what kind of lives we might have had if we had done something differently.

Those speculations don't do much good. The better solution is to discover one's place in life and make the best of it. There is enough to life around us that we can live fully and richly wherever we are.

Science fiction writer Ray Bradbury wrote a book about his summer as a 12-year-old boy in Waukegan, Illinois. He tells about Leo Auffmann, the town jeweler who made a "Happiness Machine." It looked like a telephone booth, and inside you saw pictures of famous foreign scenes on a screen and heard lovely music. When his wife went inside she first said, "Amazing," but then started crying. "It's the saddest thing in the world!" she wailed. "I feel awful, terrible." She explained that she would never see all these wonderful places. She called it a "Sadness Machine," because it tempted her to think that happiness was in places far away from her home and family.

Leo realized she was correct. Later that night he motioned to his father-in-law, "You want to see the *real* Happiness Machine? The one they patented a couple thousand years ago? It still runs, not good all the time, but it runs. It's been here all along . . . " He pointed to the front window and whispered, "Here . . . Quiet, and you'll see it." They peered through the large windowpane.

There, in small pools of lamplight, they saw Saul and Marshall, playing chess at the coffee table. In the dining room Rebecca was laying out the silver. Naomi was cutting paper-doll dresses. Ruth was painting watercolors. Joseph was running his electric train. Through the kitchen door, Lena Auffmann was sliding a pot roast from the steaming oven. You could hear someone singing in a high sweet voice. You could smell bread baking, too, and you knew it was real bread that would soon be covered with real butter. Everything was there and it was working.

"There it is," Leo said, "the Happiness Machine."[4]

It was his own family, living their everyday lives together. Happiness was not far away in Paris, Rome, or Egypt, but in his own home. We don't need a machine, television or movies to transport us around the world to find happiness. The stuff of life which makes joy is all around us every day. The Christian view of our vocation in God's world makes it crystal clear how the meaning and fullness of life is found not in exotic, far-away places, but right where we are, with the people around us.

4. Ray Bradbury, *Dandelion Wine* (New York: Alfred A. Knopf Publishing, 1975), 69–71.

A FENCE OR A ROADMAP?

The very first question in Shorter Catechism of the 1649 *Westminster Standards* is: "What is the chief end of a human being?" The answer is: "A human being's chief end is to glorify God and to enjoy him forever!"

Enjoy God? Yes, life with God is meant to be joyous!

Many people think that the good life is the freedom is "do anything I want." They imagine that being a Christian and following God's laws take all the fun out of life. Such persons think of Christianity as a *fence*. They think Christianity puts up boundaries, limiting what one can do and taking all the enjoyment from life.

God's law is actually more like a *roadmap*. The Ten Commandments are a guide for truly happy and fulfilling human life. The stone tablets that Moses received from God were instructions on how to live. They can be summed up by saying, "Love God and love others, and life will go well." "Honor your parents; do not kill, commit adultery, steal, lie, or covet"—that's good advice for happy living for everybody! Disobey them and trouble is inevitable.

God's Ten Commandments are for human life, as the laws of nature are for the physical world. If you disregard the law of gravity and jump from a 10-story building, you suffer the consequences! It makes no sense to say, "I'm free to jump off here." You might be free to set off across a desert without enough food and water, but disregard those simple rules and you're done for.

If you wish to reach your destination, you follow a map. That's what God's laws are for. It's no wonder that that the very first psalm in the Bible describes God's people by saying, "their delight is in the law of the Lord, and in this law they meditate day and night." (Psalm 1)

A "NEW COMMANDMENT"

How should we treat other human beings? How should we live? The Christian answer is both simple and complicated.

Religious leaders once asked Jesus, "What is the greatest commandment in the law?" It was a trick question, because there were hundreds of commandments and laws. How could one possibly single out any of them? Jesus did. He answered,

> You shall love the Lord your God with all your heart, and with all your soul, and with all your mind. This is the greatest and first commandment. (Matthew 22:37–38)

Careful listeners knew he was quoting Deuteronomy 6:5 from the Old Testament, one of the most sacred verses for Jews. Then Jesus added another verse, again from the Old Testament,

> And a second is like it: "You shall love your neighbor as yourself." (Matthew 22:39, also Leviticus 19:18)

Soon after that, when Jesus was with his disciples the day before he would be crucified, he summarized his teachings. "I give you a new commandment," he told them, "that you love one another. Just as I have loved you, you also should love one another." (John 13:34) Later on John wrote in his Epistle, "This is what love is, not that we love God, but that God first loved us and sent his Son to be the sacrifice for our sins." The next verse gives the consequences: "Since God loved us so much, we also ought to love one another." (1 John 4:10–11)

The Apostle Paul put it in a nutshell:

> For the whole law is summed up in a single commandment, "You shall love your neighbor as yourself." (Romans 13:9–10, also Galatians 5:14)

Boil down all the commands and laws of the Bible, and that's the one-word summary: Love.

Christian love is far more than romantic love. It is a deep respect for the worth and dignity of every human being. The pattern was set by Jesus, who loved and cared for all people, even those shunned by the rest of society. To live with Jesus is to love as Jesus did.

The goal is clear and simple, but living it can be complicated. Loving others is not always easy. By our nature we are self-centered creatures. We think first of ourselves and sometimes fail to take the next step of thinking about others.

Furthermore, we are constantly bombarded with decisions where it is not clear what the loving way to act is. Sometimes a loving parent must discipline a child. An employer has to dismiss someone who cannot do the job. Teachers flunk students who don't hand in their work. People who want to do the right thing often disagree on what course of action is best. Ethical and political issues are extremely complicated. Sometimes we have to choose between two options, and we aren't sure which is better.

And yet, the overall vision remains constant: Love one another. Despite the complications, it's the wonderful, shining goal for human life!

11

Why the Church?

The church has taken some hard knocks in the last half century. Many people are disappointed in traditional church life and have dropped out, even though they consider themselves Christian. Some of this disappointment is deserved, since there are plenty of times people in churches have not lived up to what the church aspires to be.[1]

"CHURCHLESS" CHRISTIANS?

PAUL RAJASHEKAR, professor at the Lutheran Seminary in Philadelphia, summarizes the problem:

> ... there are millions of people in Western societies who claim to be Christian, albeit "churchless Christians." ... These "churchless Christians" seem to be estranged and disillusioned with established churches and have sought alternative forms of community.[2]

---

1. Frederick Buechner, *The Clown in the Belfry. Writings on Faith and Fiction* (San Francisco: Harper, 1992), 1.

2. "Parish Practice Notebook," Lutheran Theological Seminary in Philadelphia, Spring 1996, 1.

Statistics tell us that about 90% of Americans believe in God, but only about 65% of the population belongs to a church or synagogue and less than half of them attend a worship service on any given week. Millions of people are very interested in "religion," but not in the "church."

A thoughtful high school boy once announced to me that he was going to "be a Christian on my own," as he said. He liked the term "lone-wolf Christian." He was on a church committee and felt the group frittered away their time on trivial matters, and he was correct. He thought his faith would grow better if he did it on his own. He told me that his first project was to read the Bible cover to cover.

I wished him well. I suggested that as he read the Bible he keep an eye open for those people who cultivate their faith and religious life by themselves. Some weeks later I asked him how the Bible reading was going. He said he had just finished. I asked if he remembered my suggestion, and he replied sheepishly that he never found anybody in the Bible who lived alone in his or her faith. He began to rethink his attitude toward the church.

"I" AND "WE"

We often speak of Jesus as "*my personal* savior," and that is true. I have a "personal" relationship with God, because God knows who I am and deals with me as an individual. My faith is also uniquely "my own," because it has been shaped by my own experiences and convictions, which are different from any other person's.

Faith is intensely personal, but it also makes us a part of a community or family as a church. Jesus is not only *my* savior, but he is also the savior of every other believer, and we are bound with other believers in that faith. Most churches use two creeds in their worship services. The Apostles' Creed says "*I* believe . . . ," and the Nicene Creed says, "*We* believe . . . " Both are true and necessary.

We already noted that the one prayer Jesus taught us begins with "*Our* Father," not "*My* Father." There is no *I, me* or *my* in the Lord's Prayer, only *our* and *us*. Even when we pray it by ourselves, we are praying to God as part of a larger family.

WHY THE CHURCH?

The simplest answer to "why the church?" is: To be a disciple of Jesus connects me to other believers. Life with God means life with others. Do you want to experience God? Spend time with other Christians. Faith makes us a community or a family.

One of the deepest human needs is to belong, to be connected to other people, to be part of a community. That is true on a human level, and it is true on the level of faith as well. God's plan for humanity is to draw us together, to break down the barriers which separate us.

It would be impossible to function as a Christian without the church. People can do things together which they cannot do as scattered individuals—send missionaries, support schools here and abroad, maintain homes for the elderly, coordinate aid to third world countries, publish educational materials, hymnbooks, and so on. Paul describes the church as the "body of Christ," a body with eyes, ears, hands and feet—all different but working together as a living body together.

Most importantly, Christians worship together. Coming together with people of faith strengthens our own faith. Presbyterian pastor John Ackerman told about a young woman who had trouble believing in anything during her years of mental illness:

> She remembered the darkest times, and said that going to church helped on days when she couldn't believe. She was buoyed up by the faith of others. When she couldn't say, "I believe in God almighty," she could hear others say, "We believe … "[3]

I will never forget a Sunday morning when I was alone in Germany as a foreign student. I decided to attend a church service on a U.S. Army base, with no idea what denomination it was or what kind of service it would be. The chaplain began the service with the call to confession:

> Beloved in the Lord, let us draw near with a true heart and confess our sins unto God our Father, beseeching him in the name of our Lord Jesus Christ to grant us forgiveness …

These were the same words that began our Sunday service back home. I was thousands of miles away from my home and family, but the impact of "being home" with those words was so overpowering that I stood with tears running down my face. I didn't know one person in that army chapel, but I was with my family again through worship.

I can feel close to God by myself, but feeling the presence of God can be so much stronger when we're with others who are worshipping God. I can sing a hymn by myself at home,

3. Sermon at Westminster Presbyterian Church, Minneapolis, Minnesota, May 28, 1989).

but it is much more meaningful (and sounds a whole lot better!) when my voice is joined with others. I can pray my own concerns to God, but when I am in church my horizons are widened as I join in prayer for people and concerns I would not have known about by myself.

I remember the first time I attended a conference of Christians from around the world. As we began with the Lord's Prayer I was standing between a Dutch monk in his brown Franciscan robe and a woman from Indonesia. We prayed each phrase of the Lord's Prayer in our own languages. They were total strangers to me, and except for the closing "Amen" I didn't understand a syllable of what they were praying. But from that moment on we no longer thought of ourselves as strangers. We were brothers and sisters in Christ, as powerful a tie as any friendship or family.

THE COMMUNION OF SAINTS

Being part of the church connects us with all the Christians who have lived before us. One of my favorite Bible passages is Hebrews 12: "Therefore, since we are surrounded by so great a cloud of witnesses . . . " Imagine a cheering section of people in heaven, the "cloud of witnesses" surrounding us with encouragement from their celestial vantage point. We are uplifted by the thought that the saints in heaven are connected to us as a "cloud of witnesses."

Some people considered the new sanctuary of Vinje Lutheran Church in Willmar, Minnesota, disturbingly modern when it was built in 1962. Traditional churches were built in the shape of a cross. The Willmar congregation surprised people by building a circle. The theme inscribed in the sanctuary is "Therefore, since we are surrounded by so great a cloud of witnesses ... " To emphasize this message, many names of this great band of witnesses are inscribed on the wall all around the sanctuary. They start with Adam and Eve and other Old Testament figures—Noah, Abraham, Sarah, Moses—then add the disciples of Jesus, with Mary and Martha, followed by great persons from church history—Paul, Augustine, Thomas Aquinas, and Luther. The list finishes with modern Christians—Bonhoeffer and Berggrav. The last name on the list is Ordass, the intrepid Lutheran bishop of Communist-ruled Hungary. After his name there is an empty space. I asked the church secretary, Phyllis Coleman, why that space was left. "That's the space for two more names," she answered, "yours and mine."

It's impossible to be a Christian all by yourself, even if there are times you might feel alone. We are part of this vast company of God's people, stretching back to Adam and Eve. Your name and my name belong in the circle with the rest of them.

ONE AND MANY

Why is the church divided into so many denominations? The answer to that is spread over a lot of past history. In brief, among Christians there are differences in various matters of doctrine and organization. The three main Christian groups in the world are Roman Catholics, Orthodox and Protestants.

There have been times when Christians have fought wars over these differences, sad and shameful chapters in church history.

On the other hand, church history in the last century has been marked by the "ecumenical movement," a growing sense of unity and cooperation among churches. We are divided into various denominations according to what we believe, and we respect those differences. The deeper truth is that we regard each other as brothers and sisters under God. Relations among churches are totally different now from what they were even a hundred years ago, and it has been a huge blessing for Christians around the world!

WORD AND SACRAMENT

Since its beginnings Christian worship has revolved around the Word and the Sacraments. The Word is the message of the Gospel, the "good news" of what God has done and is doing for us. This Word comes to us through the reading of the Bible, the sermon, the words of the hymns and other words spoken. In addition to the Sunday service, our faith is nurtured by words spoken to us in Sunday School, at home, or any time and any place where the Christian faith is spoken of.

The Sacraments are different. Consider for a minute what Baptism and Holy Communion do, and it will become clear why the church treasures Sacraments so highly.

1. Sacraments convey God's presence to us in a very real, concrete way. They use something visible and tangible—water, bread, and wine—with the promise that as surely as we can feel, touch, smell, and taste these things, so real is God with us. Of course God is with us through the Word and in the Spirit, but Sacraments reinforce this presence with these tangible, touchable means.

2. The fact that God comes to us in earthly elements shows the high regard God has for this world. One might expect God to use precious and expensive items as symbols of God's presence—gold, jewels, expensive foods—but no!, God comes to us through everyday household items. Water, bread and wine were the most ordinary things in any household of Jesus' time. Wine is not served in every household now, but in Jesus' time water was not reliably pure, so wine was the usual beverage.

3. The elements used in Sacraments symbolize the very meaning of the Sacraments. Water washes and gives life. Bread and wine or grape juice nourish us. Through the Sacraments we are washed, given life, and nourished in faith. One does not have to be a PhD or trained theologian to understand Sacraments. Every child understands how we need washing, eating and drinking.

There are many differences in how various churches understand and give the Sacraments. Each church or denomination has its own beliefs and practices. Are there two, three, or seven Sacraments? Who administers Sacraments? The questions are endless and complicated. Yet the large majority of Christians agree that Sacraments are gifts from God and are important for Christian faith and life. We can appreciate the beliefs and practices of others, even though they might be quite different from our own.

We experience God when we hear the words of the gospel. We experience God in concrete and touchable ways when we feel the water of Baptism and taste the bread and wine in Holy Communion. God is right there, coming to us!

BAPTISM

Jesus did not invent Baptism. John the Baptist was baptizing before Jesus came along, and other religions have similar rites. But Jesus transformed baptism and gave it new meaning. John himself pointed to Jesus and said, "I baptize you with water for repentance, but one who is more powerful than I is coming after me . . . He will baptize you with the Holy Spirit and with fire." (Matthew 3:11)

Jesus was baptized by John as the beginning of his ministry. Christians believe that something new begins when we are baptized.

1. Just as water is necessary for life, being baptized means that we receive new life in God.

2. Just as water is used for washing, so Baptism is a washing, where God washes away our sin and guilt.

3. Just as people can be drowned in water, we are drowned in Baptism. Then we are "born again" in Baptism. The Apostle Paul wrote,

> Do you not know that all of us who have been baptized into Christ Jesus were baptized into his death? Therefore we have been buried with him by baptism into death, so that, just as Christ was raised from the dead by the glory of the Father, so we too might walk in newness of life. (Romans 6:3–4)

Baptism signifies the dynamics of the Christian faith: We die or drown to sin, then are reborn through the resurrection of Jesus. In some parts of the Christian church, a child is given a new name at Baptism, to signify this new identity in Baptism.

4. Just as water is the most common liquid on earth, present everywhere, so in the same way God is present with us where ever we go. As surely as God's Spirit was with Jesus when he was baptized, so God has promised to be with each person who is baptized.

5. Just as Jesus began a new kind of life when he was baptized, so in Baptism we accept for ourselves or for our children the ideals and goals of Christian living. We are baptized "into Christ." Paul wrote to the church in Corinth:

> So if anyone is in Christ, there is a new creation: everything old has passed away; see, everything has become new! (2 Corinthians 5:17)

6. Just as we are washed clean in Baptism and brought into the mercy of God, so we are joined with other baptized persons. In Baptism we become part of God's family, the Christian church.

Christians don't agree on the age of Baptism. Most churches baptize infants soon after birth, believing that the meaning of Baptism applies also to children. Some churches wait until later, when a person can confess his or her own faith, because they see the statement of one's own faith as essential to Baptism.

Another difference of opinion is about how the water is applied. Some put the water on the head, others immerse the entire body in the water.

In spite of these differences, the vast majority of Christian churches consider Baptism as a rite which signifies with water what it means to be a Christian. All Christian churches acknowledge that Baptism is part of Jesus' "Great Commission" to the church, his last advice before ascending to heaven:

> Go therefore and make disciples of all nations, baptizing them in the name of the Father and of the Son and of the Holy Spirit . . . (Matthew 28:19)

THE LORD'S SUPPER, HOLY COMMUNION

Christians believe that Jesus lives within and among us because he assured his disciples that "where two or three are gathered in my name, I am there among them." (Matthew 18:20) On his last night with his disciples he promised them that God's Spirit will be with them. (John 16:7) After his resurrection, before he left them to ascend to heaven he promised them (and us), " . . . and remember, I am with you always, to the end of the age." (Matthew 28:20)

His presence is more than just thinking about him. He left us with a sign that conveys how surely he is with us. It is the Sacrament of the Lord's Supper.

Each spring Jewish families celebrate the Passover with a "Seder" supper. During the meal they recite the story of the first Passover and the "Exodus" after 400 years of slavery in Egypt. The family drinks wine and eats bread together, as they give thanks to God for this liberation. When Jesus ate his "Last Supper" with his disciples, the evening before he was crucified, he took bread and wine and transformed the Seder ceremony into something new. Just as the lamb was sacrificed among the Israelites before their Exodus from Egypt, now Jesus has become for us the Passover Lamb, sacrificed that we might have life. His "Last Supper" before his death became the church's "Lord's Supper" or "Holy Communion."

Through the centuries of church history there have been disagreements and controversies about the Lord's Supper—how to explain Jesus' "presence," how often to receive it, what sort of bread to use, wine or grape juice, who distributes, how to distribute, and so on. In spite of the debates, all Christians agree that in Holy Communion we experience Jesus' presence with us in a special way.

Both Baptism and the Lord's Supper emphasize how faith binds us together in this great, world-wide, eternal family, the Christian church. With this assurance, we live in the confidence that we are never alone—no matter what might happen to us, or wherever we might be.

12

What About Heaven?

> A person who works in a cancer unit told me: "I like to know the end of the story before reading the book or watching a movie. I work in a hospital with people who are very sick. With all the sadness and suffering as part of my daily life, I need to balance that with hope. I want to know beforehand if a book or movie will end happily."

IF THE topic of this book is faith in God and the experience of God in our life today, why should we think about the distant future after we die? The answer is that our faith in the future shapes very much how we live today.

THE END OF THE STORY

Experiencing God is reinforced when we know what God has in store for our future.

In the first centuries after Jesus' life, Christians were fiercely persecuted. Many died rather than deny their faith. Yet today more Christians are suffering for their faith than ever before in human history. What sustained those early Christians? What keeps Christians going today during persecutions? They are strong because they believe that they are already part of God's eternal kingdom. Knowing the end of the story helps us stand tall in this life.

About the end of the first century, an elderly Christian named John was exiled to Patmos, a small island in the Aegean Sea. There he saw visions, and his description of them became the last book in the Bible, the Book of Revelation. Much of the Book of Revelation is unclear to us, but the purpose and message of the book are crystal clear to those early Christians and to Christians ever since: *When this earth comes to its end, Jesus will stand at the end of history and reign as Lord of all!* The last two chapters conclude with a magnificent, sweeping vision of the end of time:

> Then I saw a new heaven and a new earth; for the first heaven and the first earth had passed away, and the sea was no more. And I saw the holy city, new Jerusalem, coming down out of heaven from God. (Revelation 21:1, 2.)

Yes, we know the end of the story!

SPECULATION

A short time ago a tabloid newspaper at a grocery check-out counter carried this headline:

WORLD WILL END SEPTEMBER 27

A California radio preacher made this bold announcement. The tabloid paper probably made a handsome profit from that issue, but September 27th came and went uneventfully.

Predictions are regularly made about the end of the world, and so far they have all been wrong. Bookshelves are full of books predicting future events, and people buy them as fast as they're printed. The recent *Left Behind* books sold by the millions. People look beyond the Bible for answers. You would think that in our modern scientific age, such things as astrology and horoscopes would die out, but no, they're going as strong as ever.

Why are these speculations so popular? It's because people are naturally curious about the future. This is particularly true in our uncertain world, when the very future of human civilization is constantly under the threat of nuclear catastrophe or other weapons of mass destruction.

Do you sometimes worry that some huge catastrophe will cut short your life? We all do. Especially since September 11, 2001, we are aware of the possibilities for large-scale disasters all around us.

RESURRECTION!

"Treasures of Venice," an exhibition of paintings by Venetian artists, toured the USA. One picture was a life-sized 1694 painting by Gregorio Lazzarini entitled "Faith, Hope and Love." It portrays three figures, each with a symbol to illustrate one of the three title words. The figure of faith stands in front of a cross. The figure of love is tending children around her. Those are obvious symbols. What object or symbol should an artist use to symbolize hope? Lazzarini thought of a perfect one: The third person is holding an anchor.

How do we know there is eternal life? The Christian answer is very simple: We have hope because Jesus rose from the dead. It is the anchor upon which the Christian's hope is based. The Apostle Paul was very definite:

> If Christ has not been raised, your faith is futile and you are still in your sins . . . But in fact Christ has been raised from the dead . . . so all will be made alive in Christ." (1 Corinthians 15:17, 20, 22)

We hear speculations about life after death all around us. Books are written by people who have had "near death" experiences. Their hearts stop beating, and they are clinically dead. Thanks to modern medicine, physicians restart the heart. The person wakes up and reports having gone through a tunnel of light during those moments of clinical death. Details vary, but many people have reported similar experiences.

Do such reports *prove* eternal life or heaven? Not by scientific standards of "proof." Many people consider them strong evidence for some kind of life or consciousness after death. Others think such visions are instances of oxygen deprivation during those moments when the heart isn't pumping blood to the brain.

These stories are interesting, but the Christian confidence in eternal life is not based on them. The heart of the Christian faith is that God raised Jesus back to life after he was crucified. *That* is our confidence, our anchor, in life after death!

CONFIDENCE

The 16th century French author Francois Rabelais was a Benedictine monk and a physician, but he also had a strong streak of skepticism. It is reported that his last words before dying were, "I am going away to the 'Great Perhaps.'"

Faith in the resurrection changes the "perhaps" to a "yes!"

Look around an old cemetery. Many tombstones will have expressions of confidence in eternal life. In Boston's old "Granary Burying Ground" there is a gravestone marked "David Mosely, died Jan. 6, 1818, aged 68 years." Above the inscription is one simple carving: a hand, with the index finger pointing up.

The most common symbol in the colonial cemeteries of Boston is a skull with a wing on each side, a graphic combination of a symbol of death and a symbol of eternal life.

Benjamin Franklin composed the epitaph for his own tombstone. His grave in Philadelphia's Christ Church cemetery reflects his profession as a printer, his wry wit, and his confidence in eternal life:

> The Body of
> B Franklin Printer,
> (Like the Cover of an Old Book
> Its Contents torn out
> And stript of its Lettering & Gilding)
> Lies here, Food for Worms.
> But the Word shall not be lost;
> For it will (as he believ'd) appear
> once more,
> In a new and more elegant Edition
> Revised and Corrected
> By the Author.

Retired Presbyterian pastor Donald Meisel tells of a deacon's prayer he heard in an African American church, which ended this way:

> Now, Lord, when the time comes for me to go into
> my dying room to come out no more, when the

> battle has been fought and the victory won, meet
> me down by the river where they ain't no bridge.
> Tell River Jordan to behave itself so we can cross
> over in a calm time.
> We'll get on board the old ship Zion and go reeling
> and rocking into the Kingdom of Heaven.
> Meet us where we'll sit at the feet of the angels and
> we'll look upon the sweet face of Jesus and bathe
> our weary souls in the seas of the heavenly rest.
> This is your servant's prayer.
> So I hope. So may it be, Amen and Amen.[1]

Sojourner Truth was a former slave who traveled around the country preaching and working against slavery. When she fell ill more than a hundred years ago, a friend worried that she would not recover. The gallant woman smiled and answered, "I'm not going to die, honey; I'm going home like a shooting star!" That kind of confidence spills over into everyday life!

PILGRIMS

"I'm going home," is how many Christians describe what happens whey they die. Malcolm Muggeridge, the sharp-tongued editor of the British magazine *Punch*, became a Christian as an adult. When he described the process of conversion, he wrote

> I just struggled along feeling from the beginning
> convinced of one thing, which I think perhaps
> is the basic nature of religious faith, that in this
> world I am a stranger. I don't belong here. I am
> staying here for a bit and it's a very nice place, and

---

1. Sermon, Oct. 25, 1987, Westminster Presbyterian Church, Minneapolis.

> interesting place, but I don't belong here. From the beginning I can remember that feeling and I have it still.[2]

The feeling he's describing is that of a pilgrim, one who is on a journey. Our life on this earth is a pilgrimage to our true home in God's kingdom.

We speak of 'nostalgia' as a longing for the past. When Dr. Ronald Bridges retired as president of the Pacific School of Theology, he made a suggestion in his final report to the school's trustees that "there should be a word that is the opposite of 'nostalgia,' which would denote a fond longing for the future instead of a longing for the past." He thought that 'futalgia' would be a fine addition to the English language!

One of the great Christian leaders in the 20th century was Pope John 23, whose papacy inspired sweeping changes in the Roman Catholic church. Shortly before he died of cancer, the people near him heard his last words, "My bags are packed. I'm ready to go." And then, very softly, he said, "Let us go into the house of the Lord," and with his last breath he went.

GRIEF

William Sloane Coffin, Yale University chaplain and later pastor at Riverside Church in New York City, lost his 24-year-old son Alexander in a car accident during a storm. Ten days after the funeral he spoke about his anguish in a sermon:

---

2. Malcolm Muggeridge, *The End of Christendom* (Grand Rapids MI: Wm. B. Eerdmans Publishing Co., 1980), 29.

> The reality of grief is the absence of God—"My God, my God, why hast thou forsaken me?" . . . the psalm only begins that way, it doesn't end that way. As the grief that once seemed unbearable begins to turn now to bearable sorrow, the truths in the "right" biblical passages are beginning once again to take hold: "Cast thy burden upon the Lord and he will strengthen thee"; "Weeping may endure for a night, but joy comes in the morning"; . . . "The light shines in the darkness, and the darkness has not overcome it."
>
> And finally I know that when Alex beat me to the grave, the finish line was not Boston Harbor in the middle of the night. If a lamp went out, it was because, for him at least, the Dawn had come.[3]

Faith in eternal life does not diminish grief when it hits you personally. Losing a family member or friend is a terrible experience of separation and loneliness. No one should ever say, "You don't have to grieve, because you believe in heaven." Grief cuts like a knife no matter what faith you have. Maybe grief for the Christian is even more painful than for others. If we love each other as Jesus asks us to do, then the pain of death is all the more intense.

We Christians grieve, but our faith gives us a powerful resource of healing in times of grief.

Christian hope for eternal life is not escapism. Christians do not withdraw from the joys of this world because they are waiting for joy in eternity. But our anticipation of heaven

---

3. William Sloane Coffin, *Yankee* magazine, December 1983, 168–69.

means that even in grief we still find joy in living. Following the death of his wife, Swiss physician Paul Tournier reflected:

> Now, with my new bereavement, my link with heaven is made stronger still, and that stimulates, rather than diminishes, my interest in the problems of this world . . . I can truly say that I have a great grief and that I am a happy man.[4]

That's the anchor for our hope, which gives happiness even in the midst of deep grief. We hold to that anchor every day and in every circumstance.

---

4. Paul Tournier, "The Blessings of a Deep Loss," *Christianity Today*, November 23, 1984, 28.

13

The Adventure of It All

> To fall in love with God is the greatest of all romances,
> to see Him the greatest adventure,
> to find Him the greatest human achievement.
>
> —St. Augustine, A.D. 354–430

AUGSTINE KNEW what he was talking about. His mother Monica was a devout Christian, but while growing up, Augustine tried different religions and different philosophies, all the while living a life of pleasure. Finally he met other Christians and became a disciple of Jesus. At the age of 33 he became a Christian. He went on to become one of the leading bishops and scholars of the church. He had discovered that being a disciple of Jesus was the greatest adventure of them all.

A VISION

People need a vision in life, something to fire their imagination and give them something to strive for. Our ideals in the USA are shaped by the vision of freedom and equality won in the Revolutionary War, as well as other great moments in our history. Other countries have their stories of struggles and triumphs. In Britain even the legends of King Arthur and Robin Hood continue to stir people's spirits.

The Christian faith gives us a vision both for this life and for life eternal. What greater vision for society can there be than one where "justice rolls down like waters and righteousness like an everlasting stream"? (Amos 5:24) To the question "What does the Lord require?" the prophet Micah answers, "to do justice, love kindness and to walk humbly with your God." (Micah 6:8) Jesus told us that the two great commandments were to love God and love others. (Matthew 22:36–39) James writes that true religion is to "care for widow and orphans." (James 1:27) The prophet Zechariah says that God wants us to "render true judgments, show kindness and mercy to one another; do not oppress the widow, the orphan, the alien, or the poor." (Zechariah 7:9,10) Imagine what society would be like if these wonderful visions were realized!

Those are the visions to which we strive. Are they impossible to achieve? Probably so for society as a whole, since evil is always present among humans. But Christians stake their lives on these goals.

And what a ride it can be! Christians live with those visions and work toward them. We swim upstream in society, where other forces are at work to make the rich richer and poor poorer, where corruption and injustice find their ways into places of influence, where selfishness and greed are always at work, where prejudice is often deeply ingrained in people's hearts, and so on.

It's not easy to live with the Christian vision. But it's always an adventure.

BUMPS ALONG THE WAY

A few years ago on the north shore of Lake Superior in northern Minnesota, a sign along Highway 61 read "Enjoy Your Trip—Happy Motoring." Less than a hundred feet further another sign warned "Bumps—Next 20 Miles."

Those signs could symbolize Christian life. It's an enjoyable trip with a lot of happy motoring, but there are always bumps along the way. There may even be more bumps for Christians, since God has a way of adding new concerns to life—concern for the well-being of others and for those who have less.

When Mao Tse Tung and the Communists took over China in 1949, the Christians were severely persecuted. Communication to the outside world was limited. In 1972 some Americans received an unusual message from China, saying that the "this I know people" were doing well. The Chinese authorities thought the message was nonsense, so they let it through. The Americans recognized immediately that the phrase came from Anna Warner's beloved hymn, "Jesus Loves Me, This I Know." The Chinese Christians were telling everyone that they were still steadfast in their faith. When the rigid intolerance of the Chinese Red Guard's "Cultural Revolution" was relaxed in the 1980s and Chinese Christians were allowed to worship in public again, the outside world was astonished to discover there were more Christians in China than in 1949, when the persecutions began.[1]

The confidence of God's presence always with us enables us to become more than we would be otherwise. Phillip Brooks was a great American preacher in the 19th century,

---

1. Church History Institute's *Glimpses*, Issue 62.

although he is best known as the author of the Christmas carol, "O Little Town of Bethlehem." He gave this advice for daily prayer:

> *Do not pray for easy lives; pray to be stronger men and women. Do not pray for tasks equal to your powers; pray for powers equal to your tasks. Then the doing of your work shall be no miracle, but you will be a miracle. Every day you will wonder at yourself, at the richness of life which has come to you by the grace of God.*

It is a wonderful vision of what life can be!

People who stand for something often suffer more than others. Life in this world can be very cruel, particularly if you stand for something. Some Christians suffer a great deal, others might only be teased for being a Christian.

FAITH CHANGES EVERYTHING

Peter Storey is a retired Methodist bishop of South Africa. He was the chaplain of the Robben Island prison, where Nelson Mandela was jailed for twenty-seven years. When Mr. Mandela was freed and became the president of South Africa, he appointed Bishop Storey to organize the "Truth and Reconciliation" commission, to heal the wounds left from years of apartheid. The commission's work was a truly remarkable story of applying the Christian principles of honesty and forgiveness. When he visited the United States he spent time at one of the Methodist seminaries in the USA. I asked him why he picked that school, and he replied, "Because there they really believe that Jesus changes lives."

Faith does change lives. The first step of Alcoholics Anonymous is to acknowledge that "our lives had become unmanageable" due to alcohol. How can a person conquer addiction? The second and third steps of AA are:

2. Came to believe that a Power greater than ourselves could restore us to sanity.

3. Made a decision to turn our will and our lives over to the care of God as we understood him.

After the collapse of the Soviet Union, leaders in Russia asked American AA members to come and help them with the crippling effects of alcoholism. However, they added, since Russia has been officially atheistic for so many years, their treatment of addiction could not mention God. The Americans replied that they could not help, since the only way their life was changed was when they met and believed in a higher power.

Faith can do that, and it has done so for millions of people. Faith gives courage in times of sickness or trouble; faith gives hope in times of despair; faith gives direction in times of uncertainty; faith gives joy in times of sadness, and on and on. Faith doesn't solve all problems, but it helps us see beyond them.

Charles Colson was a lawyer in Richard Nixon's White House until he spent seven months in prison for his involvement in Watergate. During this time he astonished friends and foes alike by becoming a Christian. He encourages people seeking for faith to read the Bible with this precaution:

> But be warned: Unless you are prepared to have your comfortable notions uprooted, you may want to stop reading right now... That [the Bible] is radi-

> cal stuff. It is irresistibly convicting. It is the power of God Word and it is, all by itself, life-changing.[2]

He knows from experience what he is writing about. His new faith sent his life into a totally new and dramatic direction. Now he devotes his life to Christian ministry in prisons.

VOCATION

In the Middle Ages, the word "religious" described those who joined the clergy or a religious group, such as the Franciscans, Dominicans, Sisters of Mercy, Ursuline nuns, or one of the dozens of other such groups. The common opinion was that a really devout Christian became a "religious," a priest, monk or nun. That was your "vocation," your calling to a religious life.

In the 1500s the Protestant Reformation changed this way of thinking. The Reformers defined "vocation" as one's *calling*, one's place in all areas of living. God created mankind to live in the world, and God calls us to fit into society in many ways for the good of the human family and the world. We all have several vocations in our lives—child, parent, relative, citizen, student, employer, employee, and so on. We serve God in these vocations. Our vocation is not just what we do in church—usher, teach Sunday school, sing in the choir, or whatever. We serve God Monday through Saturday as businesspersons, teachers, mechanics, lawyers, carpenters, repair persons, grocery clerks, neighbors, citizens, parents, children, and so on.

---

2. Charles Colson, *Loving God* (Grand Rapids MI: Zondervan Publishing House, 1983), 40–41.

If you ask people, "What do you do as a Christian?" they would probably answer something like, "I go to church and I'm on the youth committee there." That's correct, but that's only a small part of the answer. You could just as well answer, "I teach junior high," "I run a flower shop," or "I'm raising children." *Every role* we have in life is part of being a Christian. Your whole life is lived with God. You serve and follow God in all your vocations.

It can be complicated. At times we have to make choices, and they aren't easy. What does a parent do if a business trip is scheduled on the day of a daughter's piano recital? You have a vocation as a businessman and as a parent. What's your choice in that situation? What do you do when you have promised to help with housework and friends invite you to a movie? What do you do if the church choir is rehearsing but your grandmother needs help?

At the Lutheran World Federation assembly in Budapest, American Lutheran bishop James Crumley was an American delegate. During the meeting he received word that his brother-in-law had died. Bishop Crumley immediately flew home. He was criticized by some for letting his family affairs interfere with his duties as bishop and assembly delegate, but he responded:

> . . . My family is the place above all others where God has made me unique. No one else can fill the place for me where I relate to parents, brothers, spouse and children. Only I am Bob's son, Annette's husband, Frances' father. Here above all other human relationships do I have a particular identity. Someone else will be pastor to the people to whom I am pastor. Someone else will be a bishop of the

> church. But no one else will ever fill my place in my
> family relationships ... [3]

It's a classic statement of Christian vocation. At that time his vocation as a family member was more important than his vocation as bishop or delegate. Every one of us faces similar decisions.

Is your life important? Does God have a plan for your life? This new understanding of vocation opens up your whole life to God's guidance. Any way that you add to the well-being of other people in any of your vocations is part of God's overall plan for how creation is meant to be. Your life is a part of this grand design.

ONE CHANGED LIFE CHANGES OTHERS

Danny Wuerffel, All-American quarterback at the University of Florida, won the Heisman Trophy in 1996 as the best college football player in the nation. During that time he said, "God grabbed hold of me." He began looking for ways to make his life meaningful. While he was playing professional football with the New Orleans Saints in the National Football League, he began working with Desire Street Ministries (DSM), a group founded in 1990 to work with youth and their families in the most challenging of urban environments, a crime-ridden housing project in New Orleans. Believing that God led him into this venture, Danny Wuerffel left the NFL to become fulltime Director of Development. In a short time Desire Street Ministries accomplished the impossible—building a new church, a pediatric clinic, and a multi-million dollar high

---

3. Cited in Martin Marty's *Context* newsletter, 2–15–85.

school for boys in one of the city's most impoverished areas. Hurricane Katrina ruined the school building beyond repair, but they have already reopened the school as the Desire Street Academy.

Danny Wuerffel looks back on his football career and his Desire Street ministry as "part of God's plan, fulfilling and exciting." Once he experienced God, his life took off in a new and unexpected adventure.

His experience is one of hundreds of stories about how faith changes lives and how one changed life changes others.

THE MASTER'S TOUCH

The adventure of the Christian life comes from the powerful conviction that we are part of God's kingdom and that this great God is constantly with us. No person, no government, no power on this earth can take that away. A Christian knows that human life with God can be more creative, more wonderful, more joyous than one could ever imagine.

A story is told of the great Polish pianist Ignace Jan Paderewski. A mother took her young son to one of Paderewski's recitals, hoping to encourage the boy's progress on the piano. After they were seated, the mother walked back to greet a friend of hers in the audience. When she returned to her seat, she was puzzled to notice that her son's seat was empty. Suddenly the spotlights lit up the Steinway piano on stage, and the mother was horrified to see her son sitting at the keyboard, innocently picking out "Twinkle, Twinkle, Little Star."

Before she could move to bring him back to his seat the great pianist walked on the stage. The audience was hushed, wondering what he would do. He leaned down behind the boy and whispered into his ear, "Don't stop. Keep playing." Then Paderewski reached around the boy with his left hand and began filling in a resonant bass part. Soon his right arm reached around the other side and added a beautiful descant melody. The lad kept playing. Playing together, the old master and the young novice transformed the simple melody into gorgeous music. The audience was mesmerized.[4]

That's what happens when we experience God through faith. God reaches over our shoulder and adds melody and harmony to our lives! What a wonder! What an adventure!

---

4. Leonard Sweet, *International Christian Digest*, May 1988, 9.

www.ingramcontent.com/pod-product-compliance
Lightning Source LLC
Chambersburg PA
CBHW070914160426
43193CB00011B/1450